Profitable Customer Care

Alfred Tack

BUTTERWORTH
HEINEMANN

Butterworth-Heinemann Ltd
Linacre House, Jordan Hill, Oxford OX2 8DP

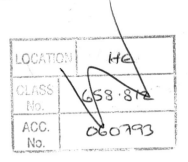 A member of the Reed Elsevier group

OXFORD LONDON BOSTON
MUNICH NEW DELHI SINGAPORE SYDNEY
TOKYO TORONTO WELLINGTON

First published 1992
Paperback edition 1994

British Library Cataloguing in Publication Data
Tack, Alfred
Profitable customer care.
I. Title
658.8

ISBN 0 7506 1882 5

Composition by Genesis Typesetting, Laser Quay, Rochester, Kent
Printed and bound in Great Britain by Clays Ltd, St Ives plc

Contents

1 Have a nice day
Alfred Tack

Visiting the hardware department of a well-known London retail store, I was treated with indifference by the assistant, who then moved to the pay desk. I was the only customer at the time, and made my way to the right of the till, where I placed my two purchases on the counter.

A brief glance from the assistant, who said, 'Will you move to the other side.'

I shrugged by shoulders, wondered a little, but then moved to the left of the till. There I waited awhile.

The assistant was evidently pondering on some weighty subject, but suddenly he said belligerently, 'I'll have to treat these two items separately!' – which he laboriously proceeded to do, while I grew more and more impatient. Eventually the transaction was concluded, and the plastic bag was handed over to me so that I could carry away the aerosol and the carpet cleaner. I had handed over my money, the assistant gave me a receipt and, in a colourless voice, said, 'Have a nice day!'

This is not a book devoted to retailing, but, because we all make purchases from shops, we do know that many assistants seem to dislike the customers intensely.

Of course customers can be difficult; but that is their prerogative. It is not the prerogative of a cashier or assistant to give bad service when confronted by an ill-mannered person. *The customer is always right* is a dictum that was the forerunner of *customer care*, which so many executives now believe is strictly adhered to in their business. Usually, it isn't!

But back to that assistant in the hardware department. You can well imagine what had happened. Someone on high had sent a memo to all members of the sales staff instructing them to end every transaction with the words, 'Have a nice day!' Whatever happened before that fond farewell doesn't matter, because all will be forgiven, believes the chief executive, if the customer is sent on his way with these good wishes. He thinks that 'Have a nice day' projects an image of a caring company.

Well, we managers do mislead ourselves on occasion, don't we! Of course chief executives have to rely on others to keep them up to date with the nitty-gritty of the business. When the chief executive walks around the store, naturally everyone is on their best behaviour. Let him disguise himself – if that were possible – and he would soon learn the truth!

People have to be motivated to give good service, and managers have to be motivated to make sure that everyone who deals directly or indirectly with customers gives 100 per cent good service. Not easy, when someone has a migraine, or an errant husband back home, or a baby in hospital!

However, a caring attitude can be achieved under nearly all circumstances, provided that an employee is adequately rewarded, and all managers are trained to understand the concepts of human relations and motivation. Then all employees will give of their best – not now and again, but all through the working day.

The key to success

The success of a customer-care programme depends almost entirely on the enthusiasm and dedication of the managing director. If the drive does not come from the top, then customer-care policies will, most surely, wither away.

It may be that Jane, the telephonist–receptionist, will be a little more understanding and polite for a while. Possibly the immediate reaction of the service manager will be to send a memo to his engineers telling them that they must now take greater care of their customers. But this only touches on the fringe of a caring outlook. Jane's efforts will quickly fade, while the service engineers will react to such memos with 'More bumph!'

The problem is that while a managing director may believe it is right that there should be a more caring attitude towards customers on the part of his workforce, he doesn't consider that such a policy is on a par with good products, excellent advertising, good marketing, good financial control, etc. That thinking results in a lack-lustre customer-care policy, because at some time everyone will say, 'It doesn't work!' But only a managing director can decide what is a priority. For example, is it cutting costs and having dissatisfied customers, or putting customer care first?

The managing director of a well-known manufacturer of white goods decided to cut service costs and switch from a direct servicing policy through agents rather than via his own engineers. Fine! But no stringent instructions were given to ensure that the agents appointed could not only give adequate service – could not only respond properly to telephone calls – but would also carry out the principles of customer care.

The result of the policy switch was lost customers and loss of market share. The managing director finally lost his job – and deservedly so – because even when irate customers wrote directly to him, he did not bother to respond. He thought all was well.

This is an example of cost-cutting that was not justified.

Another example is the electrical department of a West End London store. The store has an excellent, well-stocked department for small electrical appliances. It doesn't take long to take an electric kettle or an iron from a shelf – just a few seconds. But it can take 10 minutes or even longer to pay for it! There are always too few till assistants to help customers.

While I was there, I saw three customers replace their selection of goods on the shelves, and walk out rather than join the queue. When I queried with an assistant why this should happen, there was a shrug of the shoulders and a terse answer, 'Cost-cutting!'

Cost-cutting is essential in every business almost every day, but other aspects should be taken into account, to make sure that the cost-cutting itself does not in fact cut profits. If the managing director of that store were to visit the department, not for a walk through but to act as an assistant for an hour or two, he would return to his office and consider 'putting the customer first.'

Research has shown that seven out of ten dissatisfied customers never complain, they go elsewhere. In the world of restaurants the percentage is nine out of ten.

Customer care, however, means more than quick person-to-person service. It means that everyone in a company, whatever duties they perform, must develop a caring attitude for the customer. Otherwise the policy will fail – or achieve little success.

In another survey carried out for an engineering group it was discovered that the customers went elsewhere for these reasons:

- 14 per cent for better value.
- 22 per cent because of dissatisfaction with the product or service.
- 40 per cent because of indifferent treatment by an employee.

There were other factors, but these were the main ones.

Now let us look at the opposite side of the picture. What happens with a caring company? At the Nissan works in Sunderland the sales staff have even convinced German buyers – the toughest in the world – that the cars they purchase are as good as those built in Japan, or anywhere else in the world. Even more brilliant has been their selling cars to Japan! That's quality for you!

How did this come about? There were of course many factors, but I was told that in the main they were:

1 A continual drive for better training, in which everyone takes part and is regularly monitored.
2 A skill index monitor, with detailed charts showing the degrees of skill reached by the workforce.
3 An understanding by all managers of the basics of human relations.
4 An appreciation that people are motivated far more by a caring and understanding attitude than by autocratic management demands – 'Do this!' 'Do that!' The right motivation leads to a sense of pride throughout the workforce, with everyone striving hard to do their job better.

There can be no successful customer-care programme without training and a total quality programme, two subjects that are of course dealt with in this book. It is also directed towards managing directors, who, in the first place, must authorize a customer-care policy; and to those managers who have to carry out these instructions.

Some of the chapters have been written by executives in TACK International who are responsible for the various sessions in the Tack Customer Care courses. Their names and positions are given underneath each chapter heading. For example, Chapter 7, 'Quality customer care', is covered by Brian Moss OBE, who received this award for his chairmanship of various government committees formed to improve the quality of British products. Chapter 14, 'Time management', is written by Eric Pillinger, Managing Director of TACK International, who designed our courses in time management. You may think, 'But what has Time Management got to do with Customer Care?' Please read on, and you will discover before you reach the final chapter.

Finally, remember that the main objective of customer care is not only to enhance a company's reputation, but to increase its profits. In the business world today there is no substitute for *effective customer care*.

2 Finding quality people
Alfred Tack

Overheard:

- 'If they expect me to smile all day at customers, they can get stuffed!'
- 'Does she think she can have an engineer to call any time to suit her? And she was so bloody rude about it! I can't take much more of this!'
- 'If he sends another letter back just because he thinks it needs a minor alteration, I'll tell him what to do with his job!'
- 'I'm sorry that it's taken so long to get through, but the lines have been very busy; please don't shout at me, it isn't my fault! You'll have to be a little patient!'

All true! But you must have heard similar remarks time and time again, and then it's usually too late to attempt to put things right. A manager can only motivate, and train those who can readily accept such training and motivation. No cricket coach would give the 'go ahead' to a youngster aiming to become a professional if it was quite clear to him that the youngster had little natural talent. No impresario, producer, or director, would accept an actor or actress, or a ballet dancer, if he believed that person was seeking the impossible.

Yet managers in every sphere of activity can engage square pegs to fit into the proverbial round holes. Subsequently the reasons given are: 'You can't get good staff these days'; 'They're just not interested'; 'They only care about the money!'; 'Why are they not prepared to put in a full day's work for a full day's pay?'

I'm sure you have heard such criticisms. You may even have voiced such criticisms yourself, on occasion.

But there are other points of view concerning people in general. Here are some more quotes:

- 'You'd have thought he would stay on for a few months after all the help we've given him!'
- 'She had itchy feet, she was always looking for something better. After all, she's had five jobs in the last 10 years.'
- 'He's used us as a stepping-stone.'

There are many reasons why people want to seek other employment within months of, or a year or so after, joining a company. One main reason, however – one that is so often overlooked – originates during the initial interviewing procedure. So few interviewers tell the full truth about the position offered, in the same way as not many interviewees tell the full truth about their past when the interview is being conducted. They don't, necessarily, lie – they just gloss over the weak points. For example, to questions asked by some interviewers, such as 'Are you a hard worker?', 'Are you an enthusiast?' or 'Are you keen on this type of work?' the response invariably is 'I'm a very hard worker', 'I've always been known for my enthusiasm!' or 'It's just the type of work I've been looking for!' Such answers could come from someone who much prefers lying in bed in the mornings to arriving at the office on time, and whose enthusiasm has mainly been directed towards backing horses.

The fact that the young man (or young lady) might say to the interviewer 'I've always wanted to work in a large store like this!' need not necessarily be true, but managers untrained in interviewing and selection put such questions and accept the standard responses given as the truth. Sometimes even an experienced personnel manager, when engaging staff, does not explain everything about the job clearly, warts and all! Yet if mistakes are made at the interview stage, the result can be staff who can jeopardize the company's future by not playing their part in customer care. If they don't care about their job or their work, they will certainly not care about the customer.

The first step in customer care is to select the right staff – basically 'quality' people, who can be turned into 'high quality' people by good training. When a company is renowned for caring for its customers, you will find that every member of the staff happily plays his/her part. Without such caring attitudes management cannot succeed in its plan of winning more business, holding customers, and increasing worldwide turnover through customer care.

But let us go back to Step 1. Many, many visitors to our offices, unhappy in their work are sent by well-meaning friends or relatives for advice.

When I have asked the question, 'Why are you unhappy – you are working for a very good company?', invariably the response is, 'I was misled about the job . . .' Then follow the reasons:

- 'I was not told that some unpaid overtime was compulsory.'
- 'I was not told that I had to be pleasant to some very unpleasant customers!'
- 'It was not explained to me that although a chair was provided for me to sit down on, I should be told off if I used it.'
- 'The person who interviewed me did not explain that my territory would be cut within weeks of my joining.'
- 'I was not told that there would be so much form-filling.'
- 'I wouldn't have taken the job if I had been told that as a service engineer I was expected to look like a tailor's dummy.'

Others had expected their own office, and were upset when they had to work in a large room . . . And so the reasons why people gave up their work so quickly continued.

As I mentioned earlier, it is not possible to change

people overnight. It isn't even possible to train people to improve themselves if they are not seeking such improvement – if they think everyone is always wrong except themselves.

It is essential, when considering interviewing new applicants, to explain in detail all the good points about the job as well as those that may be more restrictive, or perhaps even unpleasant. For example, when engaging a telephone receptionist for a service department, he or she might be told something like this:

'I want to make one point clear: you will be dealing with some very difficult people – some will shout, some will bully, some will plead, some will blame you as if it's your fault, some might swear at you – but all the time, and with all callers, you will be expected to smile into the mouthpiece, and do your best to quieten them down, before explaining what you can do to help them.

This can be very difficult. It's easy to talk about it calmly now, but when you are sitting by the telephone, ready to explode with anger, and you still have to be polite, that's tough!

But of course the job has many benefits as well, because possibly 80 or 90 per cent of the people who telephone are very pleasant. I am talking about the minority.

Now think carefully. It's a good job, if you think you can take the setbacks, if you think you can make a go of it. You must make the decision. If it is 'Yes', then I'm sure you will succeed and be very happy in your work.

Some personnel managers might say, with present-day staff shortages, it's better to take rubbish than to have an empty department! I disagree. A good assistant can keep three customers happy while a poor one only loses customers. This applies to every department in an organization. A poor filing clerk will lose business. A poor receptionist will lose business. And a poor quality manager will also lose business. Only people of quality are able to put the customer first, because they are geared to do so. Such people can be found; such people can be trained to greater effectiveness. There is no reason why any manager, in any division of a company, should not be capable of engaging quality people. Managers should be trained in interviewing and selection.

Here are some guidelines.

The interview is divided into four sessions, and each session has a specific objective (see personal history form on page 35).

All applicants should be asked to complete an application form. There are three main advantages in using such a form:

(a) It enables the interviewer to assess with some accuracy whether or not an applicant should be interviewed.
(b) All applicants are judged on their answers to the same questions.
(c) The formula for interviewing is based on a completed application form. (The application form used by the TACK Personnel Selection is given on pages 35–38).

A job specification should be drawn up. Such specification is to the manager as a blueprint is to a production engineer. It sets out in detail the work to be accomplished and the duties to be carried out.

Having established the nature of the task, one must set down the type of person most likely to be able to carry it out. If someone is required to dig trenches, it is not likely that an unfit weakling can fill that position. If numeracy is essential, then anyone who has difficulty with figures would not be suitable. The specification should include:

1 Particular qualification.
2 Specific experience.
3 Educational standard.
4 A defined age range.

If a great deal of overseas travel is necessary, perhaps a single person may be preferable.

Formalizing these requirements provides standards of measurement.

The TACK interview plan

This plan comprises the following:

- Administration.
- Emphasis on preliminary interview.
- First assessment – appearance, attitude, voice, vocabulary.
- Creating confidence.
- Creating interest.
- Second assessment – applicant's reaction to terms.
- The application form page 1 – personal data.
- The application form page 2 – assessment of education, technical ability, personality.
- The application form page 3 – assessment of sales proficiency, business record.
- Questions and benefits.
- The application form page 4 – assessment of common sense, overall ability.
- The decision.

Administration

The interviewer should have the candidate's application form available, a copy of the advertisement, the man specification and the job specification.

The chairs should be placed facing each other, without a desk or table intervening. In days gone by it was usual to have cigarettes available. This is no longer necessary, unless the interviewer himself wishes to smoke.

Expenses

The method of reimbursing an applicant's expenses will depend on whether or not the interview takes place in an office or in a hotel. If in a hotel, the interviewer will probably pay the expenses himself, and the settlement should be made before the interview proper begins. If the interview is to take place in an office, arrangements should be made for a secretary, clerk, or receptionist, to pay the expenses before the interview begins.

The amount due to the applicant will already have been made clear to him in the letter arranging the appointment. The applicant knows what to expect, and if he then requests additional sums for taxis or meals when these have not been offered, it will give some indication of the applicant's character.

Notetaking

Some interviewers make copious notes. Others prefer jotting down brief comments on a specially designed form, or on the application form itself.

I believe that to make notes during the interview is discourteous to the applicant, and also unfair. Has he made a fool of himself? Has he given the wrong answer? . . .

There should be no need for these notes. Every executive should be able to retain in his memory for 30 minutes the applicant's appearance and answers to questions.

Following the interview, a few brief notes may be necessary. The question is sometimes raised, if notes are not taken, how can all the candidates be evaluated at the end of the day?

The application form itself should act as a reminder, coupled with the brief notes after each interview. Whenever possible, all interviews should take place within a day or two at the most.

No interruptions

The interviewer should ensure that there are no interruptions by telephone or personal caller during the interview.

Emphasis on preliminary interview

Why waste 30 minutes or so on an applicant when, from the moment he walks into your office, it is obvious that he will not meet the man specification so far as appearance, manner, or personality are concerned? Or again, if a little later in the interview it is clear that he does not have the vocabulary to enable him to communicate effectively?

However carefully you have vetted letters received from applicants and, subsequently, their application forms, you will still find that a high percentage of those who arrive for an interview in no way match up to their own claims. Often the man who writes the most impressive letter, and whose application form indicates that he is an applicant of outstanding ability, falls well below the standards required.

At the beginning of each interview therefore the interviewer should use such words as these:

> Mr Brown, I must begin by emphasizing that this is a preliminary interview. We have had a very large response to our advertisement (which should be true if the copy has been carefully written) and this means that although you have travelled a long way to see me, our preliminary interview will only last a relatively short time. I am sure you will agree that it is only right, in fairness to all those applicants who, like you, wrote us such good letters, that they should be interviewed. After the interviews we shall prepare a short list, when each applicant will again be interviewed, but in depth . . .

The words may be different, but the message must be

clear: do not be upset if the interview is cut short. What you do not continue to say is 'But if you impress me the interview will continue for some time'.

You have now achieved several objectives:

1 You have told the applicant that there is strong competition for the job.
2 You have enabled the applicant to 'save face' when he arrives home. Instead of being misled into believing that he has a very good chance of getting the job, he knows the odds are against him, and this he will tell his wife. Too many interviewers create the impression with a very poor quality applicant that he has been successful, and stands a good chance of getting the job. The moment the applicant leaves the office, however, NG is written across his application form. I think this is most unfair.
3 Following this explanation, you are in a position to terminate the interview quickly. In many years of interviewing I have never known anyone object to leaving after only a short interview, provided an explanation has previously been made.

First assessment – appearance, attitude, voice, vocabulary

It is almost impossible for an interviewer to decide quickly whether or not an applicant is suitable, whereas an applicant who is well below standard can be judged unsuitable within minutes. Even a relatively inexperienced interviewer will detect immediate flaws in an applicant of poor calibre.

A foolish snap judgement? Possibly! But more often than not it is a correct assessment. The advice that you will never have a second chance of making a first impression, is true of all applicants. If an applicant hasn't the common sense to set out to make a good first impression by his manner, dress, common courtesy, and tact, he will not succeed as a customer-caring employee.

Next the interviewer must make a general evaluation of the applicant.

Irrespective of the first impression – good or bad – every applicant must be listened to before the first (and, for some, the final) assessment is made. After that assessment the interview will either be cut short (in line with the apology made) or the full presentation given.

The interviewer will begin by saying, 'As I have already mentioned, this is only a preliminary interview, and as you have given me a complete CV (completed application form, or full details in your letter) I need only ask you to elaborate on one or two points. Afterwards I shall be only too pleased to answer any questions you may like to ask about our offer.'

Usually, the applicant who has already created a bad impression will not change the interviewer's opinion of him during this exercise. The average or good applicant should pass this assessment. The objective at this stage is only to cut down time-wasting with unsuitable applicants, and to make certain that you have not been unfair.

This is what you will ask him: 'Please give me in five minutes a brief outline of the work you are doing, and the reasons you now wish to change your job (or why you left your last job).' During the following few minutes the interviewer should not interrupt the applicant. If the interviewer is still uncertain after those few minutes have passed, he should allow the applicant to continue a little longer. He will then either talk himself out of a job, or persuade the interviewer that he is a man worth interviewing in some depth. If convinced, however, of the applicant's unsuitability, the interviewer should stop him at some point with: 'Thank you for answering the questions I have asked in such a short time. Now I shall be equally brief and give you further details of the job . . .'

The interviewer need then only spend a few minutes giving some facts about his offer, and close the interview.

It is important to make sure that the applicant is left with no false hopes. When saying goodbye, tell him: 'Now don't forget, there are twenty other applicants to be seen today and tomorrow. Please therefore don't be disappointed if we cannot place you on the short list . . .'

You might now ask, why not be tough and tell the applicant straight away that he is not suitable? The reason is that very few applicants can accept a refusal, and however weak they may be, they will fight hard to convince you that you are wrong. Then it is very difficult to terminate the interview. It is far better to write a letter a few days later.

If, however, you have assessed the applicant as a strong personality, you will continue by giving a full presentation.

Creating confidence

The objective of the interviewer is to win over the applicant so that he discards thoughts of all other offers he may have received. The applicant's objective is to discover whether or not the job will give him increased earnings, improved status, and greater opportunities for advancement, and whether or not he will be able to work with the interviewer (assuming that the interviewer is to be his manager).

We have therefore two men on their very best behaviour. The interviewer will claim (most do) that the job he is offering is one of near perfection. It has every advantage and no disadvantages. The opportunities are great – the possible future earnings almost astronomical. The applicant, with the fervour of a missionary, will claim to be a very hard, dedicated worker.

And so the charade continues. The applicant explains why he particularly wants to join the interviewer's organization, and the interviewer stresses that there is nothing to stop the applicant, one day, sitting in his chair.

The interviewer may believe that his time is well spent – that he has won over the applicant – but the applicant is only playing a part. As soon as he has left the interviewer, he hurries off to keep another appointment.

The interviewer has not won – he has lost. Why?

The experienced interviewer knows the first step must be to create confidence. If, at an interview, this confidence is not established, the quality applicant is unconvinced that the job is for him, and the interviewer may have to be satisfied with engaging a lower calibre person who is eager for the job. Only when the interviewer is truthful and paints a fair picture of a company, its activities, and the opportunities offered, will the quality applicant be convinced that the company is worth joining. He is not motivated by claims made in many advertisements, and by so many interviewers – claims that, they know, cannot be substantiated.

The time taken for confidence-building will depend on whether or not the applicant has previously received a brochure defining the company's activities. If he has received publicity matter, the interviewer need only say, following the first assessment, 'Thank you for being so explicit. In return let me also tell you briefly more about our organization . . .'

The interviewer, whether the applicant has received a company brochure or not, will explain in some depth the confidence-creating benefits the company can offer. For example:

> Mr Jones, I am sure you know something about our organization, but perhaps you are not aware that we have won the Queen's Award for Industry for 2 years out of the last 4. Another factor that will no doubt interest you is that our factory in Gloucester is considered to be one of the most modern production units of its kind in Europe. Let me show you some photographs . . .

Or another example to appeal to a sales engineer:

> We are a completely marketing-orientated company, which means that not only are our products right, but our back-up service is also first-class. For example, we have a service engineer in each area, and can guarantee service within 24 hours . . .

An example to appeal to the security-minded person could be:

> The point that will interest you is that we have an exceptionally low turnover of staff. You are only here because of a promotion. Our fine record in this respect is due not only to our outstanding range of products, but because of the care we take in selecting and training our staff. There is therefore very little risk of someone with all-round abilities not succeeding with us.

The confidence-creating sentences will vary from company to company, but the applicant must be convinced in the first session that the company produces quality products (or services), is sound financially, has an understanding of human relations, and offers a measure of security as well as opportunities for advancement.

If, however, the interviewer talks in terms of 'the greatest', 'the largest', 'the finest', 'the most dynamic', 'go-getting', 'great promotion possibilities', 'huge demands', he can create the reverse effect – a loss of confidence.

Creating interest

A measure of confidence having been established, the interviewer must, during the first session, interest the applicant in the job offer. This objective he achieves by asking questions: 'Mr Brown, I have told you something about our organization; what motivated you most of all to reply to our advertisement?'

The reply will indicate the lines the interviewer should

take to create interest. Here are some examples of answers given:

- 'There seems to be a very big demand for your products.'
- 'You have a very fine reputation for quality equipment. Now with my last company . . .'
- 'The opportunity for advancement.'
- 'You stressed in the advertisement that if a salesman is prepared to work hard, the rewards would be high.'
- 'I must be honest, I know we make security for ourselves, but there is always better job security with a company of your size and reputation.'

The interviewer will now know one or more of the applicant's interests, and he will build on those interests. For example:

> You were right when you said that there is a great demand for our products, Mr Brown. But it is a demand which has been created by having fine quality products and outstanding service.

Another example:

> It's nice to know that so many people are aware of our fine reputation, but it is a reputation that had to be won, and must be maintained. Let me tell you something about our design group . . .

Create interest by discovering what most interests the applicant, remembering always that the factors which do create interest are direct or indirect benefits, and it is only the benefits offered which will motivate a first-class salesman to change jobs.

Second assessment – applicant's reaction to terms

Directly after creating interest, the interviewer must give or restate the terms and conditions of employment. The interviewer can say: 'Your other interest, of course, is your potential earnings with us. Let me remind you of these. Your basic salary would be £EFG. You would be supplied with an ABC car, and additional benefits.' While you are giving these details, watch the applicant closely. If he has misunderstood the terms, or he is unhappy when he hears them for the first time, he will react by showing signs of stress. He will look away, bite his lips, change his expression, look downcast, lose his previously enthusiastic appearance. Also he will not respond quickly, and for a few moments his speech will be hesitant.

If the applicant accepts the terms and conditions, nothing more need be said. Should he show signs of dissatisfaction, however, the interviewer must ask, 'Have you any questions relevant to our pay structure?'

If the interviewer has misinterpreted the signs, the applicant who is satisfied will give an immediate favourable response. If he is dissatisfied, he will say something like this: 'I thought, perhaps, the basic would be a little higher to begin with . . .'; 'I didn't realize that I would be stationed at . . .'; or 'I thought health insurance would be included . . .'

If you believe that this applicant is worth persevering with, all his doubts must be eradicated from his mind. If not, you can cut the interview short on the lines indicated earlier.

If an applicant is unhappy with the terms, continuing with the interview is a waste of time. If he expresses doubt, in most cases you will not win him over. Even if, at the end of the interview, he seems to be keen on the job, the chances are that he will write a few days later to say, perhaps, that on handing in his notice he received such a generous offer that he could not refuse it. If ever you receive such an excuse you may be reasonably sure that the applicant never really thought he could improve his status, earning capacity, or chances of future promotion with your company.

What has been achieved so far?

1 Good administration has put the applicant at his ease, his expenses have been paid, and there have been no interruptions.
2 An apology has paved the way for the interviewer to terminate the interview quickly if necessary.
3 The applicant has been assessed for appearance, attitude, and vocabulary.
4 The interviewer has created confidence by talking in terms of the applicant's interests.
5 The applicant has been assessed on his reaction to your terms.

Now the interviewer has to assess the applicant in greater depth, while persuading him that the job offer is so good that it is worth fighting for.

The interviewer now picks up the application form or letter. The applicant should be made to feel that he has completed a form that is of great value to the interviewer – not something to be glanced at, while the interviewer is talking about his own prowess (the fault of many interviewers).

After a few moments' study, the interviewer will begin the questioning.

Will you now study pages 35–38 in which our standard application form is outlined. We can then consider the questioning of an applicant together.

The application form page 1 – personal data

The first questions put to the applicant are almost rhetorical, and, at the most, will require only a yes or no answer. For example:

'You are purchasing your own house?'
'I see you have your own car . . .'
'You are married, with three children?'

As soon as the interviewer studies the application form,

the applicant will automatically tense himself, knowing that he is about to be closely questioned.

His early yes or no answers will help to relax him. All applicants, whether highly skilled or not, are tense at some time during an interview. Some hide it, some do not, but an applicant's tension can create a wrong impression in the mind of the interviewer.

The interviewer should, during the whole interview, invite an occasional yes or no answer, either partly to relax the applicant or in order to change the pace of the interview. But in the main his questions should demand enlightenment or elaboration of answers already given on the application form. It is not possible to make an assessment on brief affirmatives or negatives.

There are several specially designed questionnaires that, supposedly, help the interviewer to ask pertinent questions. One consists of seventy-four questions. How does an interviewer memorize them? Or is he supposed to read from the list in front of him, like the after-dinner bore who reads his speech?

There is no need to memorize seventy-four questions. To refer continually to the application form is acceptable to an applicant – in fact he will expect to see his form on the interviewer's desk, and will be surprised if it is not used.

If the applicant has not completed such a form, he will expect to see his original letter on the desk. The interviewer will already have annotated the letter, to remind him of one or two points.

There is a very simple formula for enabling you to phrase questions which will help you to form a judgment of the applicant, and correctly assess his abilities. All you have to do is to remember first a few simple lead-in words. They are:

Tell me . . .
Describe to me . . .
Explain to me . . .

And, secondly, these single words:

How?
Why?
When?
What?
Which?

That's simple enough, isn't it? These are words you can memorize in less than a minute.

Let us look again at the application form, to recognize the simplicity and effectiveness of this formula:

Tell me:
What did you find most interesting in your life at university?
Why did you decide to take a course in psychology at the London Polytechnic?
What made you decide to learn the German language?
When do you write up your customer records?
Why do you write them up at that time?

Explain to me:
Which of your past managers did you most enjoy working with?
Why did you prefer working with Y rather than Z?
How do you plan your work?

You cannot fail to ask the right questions when you use the application form as a basis for this formula.

The application form page 2 – assessment of education, technical ability, personality

On the second page of the form the applicant answers questions relating to his education, further training (either technical or professional), his knowledge of foreign languages, and his leisure interests. His answers to these questions will undoubtedly give the interviewer an understanding of the personality and technical skills of the applicant.

It is during this part of the interview that the interviewer can identify himself closely with the applicant. This could result in there being a 'halo' problem. The halo, metaphorically speaking, shines over the head of the applicant with whom the interviewer has an immediate rapport – they both went to the same school or university; their technical training was on similar lines, with perhaps, a common friendship with an instructor; they both speak the same languages, and have visited the same overseas country regularly; and perhaps they have the same hobbies, such as golf or sailing.

With a friendly and warm relationship quickly established, that applicant has an advantage over other candidates. He may even be preferred to someone with greater potential than his own.

Conversely, it is sometimes difficult not to feel antagonistic towards an applicant who may, in some ways, annoy or irritate you. Possibly he smokes, when the interviewer is trying hard to forgo smoking, is too familiar, or too brusque. When interviewing, we should all be aware of our weaknesses, and not be swayed by our emotions.

The application form page 3 – assessment of sales proficiency, business record

On the third page of the application form the applicant lists his business record, information about his past employers, the nature of their business, and the length of time he was with them, etc. Very rarely, however, does an applicant fill in this record accurately.

The dates of his previous jobs may not coincide with the facts – perhaps a cover-up for non-employment over a period – and there have been cases where the applicant has served a prison sentence for embezzlement, and covered the time span by changing dates and relying on the interviewer not to check with previous employers. A standard ploy of applicants is to write in the appropriate space: 'Thinking of emigrating, we decided to spend a year in Australia, staying with relatives'; or 'I accepted a job in Canada, but we decided that we preferred to live in England'.

When these statements are made, the interviewer should question previous employers closely. He should also ask the applicant for the names and addresses of the friends or relatives, or business associates, in the countries concerned.

If the applicant really believes that enquiries will be made, he will either back down and tell the interviewer that he will send the names and addresses later, after he has checked them, and the interviewer will rarely hear from him again; or, if he has been truthful, he will supply all the evidence requested, in order to prove that he was in fact in the countries stated during these times.

Check those references

The interviewer has now reached the stage when he has to assess the applicant's ability

However experienced an interviewer may be, or whatever the results of aptitude or psychological tests the candidate may have taken, the fact is that five minutes spent talking to his previous employers will teach you more about the applicant than, possibly, an hour's interviewing. The interviewer makes judgements – but the past employer gives facts. The interviewer working though the applicant's business record will formulate opinions that may be right or wrong. The way to be certain that they are right is to check up on the applicant's statements.

Letters of recommendation that applicants show may prove useful, but they are not the complete answer. The fact that in his spare time an applicant is a lay preacher or that he spent nearly the whole of his working life with two well-known companies must not affect the decision to enquire more deeply into his background.

The applicant may have stated every relevant fact accurately, but he may not have told the truth in answer to a most important question: 'Why did you leave job A, or job B, or job C?'

The written answer will usually be:

1 Wanted to better myself.
2 My company wanted me to move to . . . but
   (a) my wife didn't want to move,
   (b) it would upset my children's education,
   (c) I didn't like the idea of living in . . .

Maybe they are all truthful statements – but maybe they are not.

Another reason often given for leaving is 'personality clash'. This could mean that the applicant has been working for a difficult manager, but the possibility is that the applicant is difficult to work with.

Another hackneyed reason is: 'They didn't keep their promises to me'. This is usually written by an applicant who has only been with his company a year or so.

Many managers act kindly towards employees who, although dismissed, may be allowed to claim that they resigned. Very rarely will an interviewer read the true reason for the applicant's 'resignation'. Few executives enjoy dismissing people. Most of them dread it. It is an admission of failure on their part.

To enable an inefficient employee to get another job, a manager will often give quite a reasonable written reference: 'Honest, hard-working, was not able to make full use of his potential with us . . .' This kind of statement can mean anything, but too often it is accepted at its face value by the interviewer, who is tired of seeing so many poor applicants.

Most written references are of little value when judging an applicant's skills.

Never write for references. Telephone, whatever the cost. When you have made contact with the referee, say something like this: 'My name is Brown of the Black & Blue Company. John Smith, who used to work for you, has applied to us for a position. Would you mind if I asked you a few questions about him? Or perhaps you would prefer to call me back – of course, on a reverse charge call . . .'

Most sales executives won't even consider the fact that it might be John Smith himself telephoning to discover what is being said about him, and will readily agree to answer the questions. A tiny minority may call back, and perhaps one in a hundred (it has never happened to me) will insist on giving a written reference only.

Have a list of questions prepared, but never invite yes or no answers. Your objective is to learn the truth, and not to be given answers that are a cover-up for inefficiency: 'Oh yes, he was quite good', or 'Oh yes, that's true, we did have to make him redundant'.

Begin by thanking the referee, whom we shall call Mr Johnson, and assuring him that if ever you can reciprocate, you will do so. At this stage you only want to verify the main statements made by John Smith. To learn the truth you must give some indication that you know the truth. If you make a wrong inference, you will be corrected, and that is a good mark for Smith.

Do not, then, ask Mr Johnson why Smith left him, but say something like this: 'I am a little concerned about Smith's statement that he left you because he didn't want to move. Somehow I felt this was not the sole reason – it didn't ring true to me. If he was as good as he says he is, I am sure you would have persuaded him to move . . .'

You will find that this type of leading question will nearly always bring the truth. Mr Johnson may possibly reply, 'Well between you and me he wasn't all that good! He has wife trouble and he was for ever taking days off or going home early. He's honest enough, mind you . . .'

You've heard enough! Smith should seek a different type of job.

Here is another way of probing for the truth: 'Smith told me that he had been promised promotion. Knowing your company I am sure that he would have achieved this promotion if he had been worth it. What held him back, Mr Johnson?'

And Mr Johnson will tell you. Very often the replies will bear out Smith's stories, and you will learn that Smith is competent but needs continual guidance.

It is always difficult to raise the question of a personality clash. For example, 'He told us there was a clash of personalities, and that if I contact you, you would not give him a very good reference.'

'You're right! He refused to report regularly – didn't agree with reporting. Also, because he enjoys camping, he would leave early every Friday afternoon. There was a clash all right!'

Who is right, the manager or Smith? If you are uncertain, then give Smith the benefit of the doubt, and telephone other past employers.

Another question which nearly always brings out the truth is: 'Mr Johnson, what did you find wrong with Mr Smith?'

More often than not you will get a reasonably good verbal reference for the applicant about whom you have little doubt, and whom you believe to be telling the truth. It is those you are not sure about – those who give you an uneasy feeling that something is not quite right – where you will generally find that your judgement is borne out by the references given.

There is one final question you can put, if still doubtful: 'Mr Johnson, would you employ Smith again?' If the answer is no, ask 'Why not?' But remember always to be polite, reasonable, and never snap out a question brusquely.

Before telephoning employers, this is what I usually say

to applicants about whom I am doubtful: 'When I telephone Mr Johnson, I am sure he will bear out everything you say. But I shall ask him this question: "What did you find wrong with Mr Smith?" Now, Mr Smith, you tell me how Mr Johnson is likely to reply to that question.' The applicant will either insist that he cannot express any views other than those already given, or he may demur for a moment or two, and then change his story, telling you the true reason for his leaving.

What you are seeking from Mr Johnson is weaknesses that are not acceptable to you: lack of loyalty, laziness, phoney absenteeism, unwillingness to give good service to customers, more interest in hobbies than in work . . . Other faults or weaknesses, however, may be quite acceptable.

When I interviewed an executive for a top position with one of our companies, he did everything right and came through the interview extremely well, but somehow I felt uneasy. I put the question to him about how I would approach his Mr Johnson, but again he insisted that Mr Johnson could not say anything derogatory about him.

I telephoned, and this was the answer I received: 'He was a very abrasive personality. He is also most argumentative, and determined to get his own way. Quite willing to break some of the company's rules, although most annoyed if called to task for not reporting on time, for example.'

I engaged the man, and he was most successful with us. Knowing his weaknesses, we were able to adopt the right tactics with him. On occasion we would humour him; at other times we would guide him, while making him believe that it was really he who was guiding us.

Another applicant I liked at the interview gave me a reason for leaving his last job that did not ring true. He told me that I should be wasting my time telephoning his previous employer, an impossible man to work for. In fact, he told me, on the day they parted they had nearly come to blows.

Normally I should have considered turning that man down on his own evidence, but he was so good in so many other ways that I thought I ought to telephone his ex-boss, and this is what he told me: 'The man's a neurotic, although undoubtedly an excellent service manager but he went to pieces after his wife left him; then he found a bird, who also left him. He was always taking time off to sort out matters, and continually wanting to borrow money. It was because I wouldn't loan him the money that in the end we had a very strong difference of opinion.'

I saw that applicant again, and invited him to tell me the real truth about his home life. On his application form he had not even hinted that he was not living with his wife. Suddenly he was glad to be able to explain everything and get it all off his chest. It was a long story he told, but he was obviously not altogether to blame – it had been fifty-fifty.

I explained to him that the problem seemed psychological, and that I had the greatest sympathy with anyone living under such stress. But I engaged him. He was with us for 7 years, succeeded, and eventually went abroad with his wife, to start a new life.

All you are seeking when you telephone past employers is the truth. Then you must decide whether or not the applicant is worth engaging.

Questions and benefits

Although in most instances you will check the applicant's credentials, you will still have to form your own judgement and make your own decisions. It is the applicant's detailed background and the manner in which he answers your questions that will determine, in the main, whether or not you will engage him. You will, therefore, question him closely on specific subjects.

This is what to look for:

1 Does he interrupt you when you are asking him a question?
2 Does he only answer the question you have put to him, or does he allow his mind to wander on to other subjects?
3 Does he bore you?
4 Does his enthusiasm for the job show?
5 Does his emotion show when he criticizes his past employers?

You may perhaps have asked him to explain once more the difficulties he experienced when working for X. A quite usual response is: 'May I be honest with you?' This presupposes that he has not been honest all along. He may then continue denigrating his past employers with a vindictiveness that, if a part of his nature, could affect his relations with his customers as well as with head office staff.

During this session, allow the applicant to talk without interruption for 3 minutes or so. If he pauses, do not help out by asking another question. Allow him to show his mental ability to continue a conversation, even under the very mild stress of not achieving a feedback from the interviewer.

Finally, probe the applicant's rigidity of thinking. Every applicant brings with him the experience gained previously. His style has perhaps developed over many years. Has he the mental ability to make changes to adapt himself to your ways of thinking?

Throughout this session, remember your twin objectives: to assess the applicant's ability, and to motivate the first-class applicant to be eager to join your company. Continue therefore to stress the benefits your company can provide.

Application form page 4 – assessment of common sense, overall ability

You will now be making your final assessment. In most interviews your decision will be made after completion of the page 4 business record. However, if you have a reservation, you should seek additional information.

Questions such as these will indicate the applicant's standard of common sense:

1 'You write that you want to succeed and obtain promotion to sales manager level. Please tell me why you believe that you can achieve your aim with our company, although you were not able to do so with your present employers.'

The weak man always pays lip service to being ambitious, and to his desire to become a sales manager, but he will give quite fatuous answers to this question. He will repeat his life story – why he failed at some jobs, but could have succeeded, except for unfairness, or the mistakes of others, never due to his own lack of ability. His answer should run on these lines: 'I have been gaining experience with every job, and I hope that I have benefited from my selling. I believe that with your company you will give me the opportunity to succeed, because . . .'

2 'You have obviously applied for other positions. I am not asking you to tell me the names of the companies you have written to during the past month or so, but will you tell me the type of product or services they are selling?'

If he has any common sense he will first explain why your advertisement attracted his attention. He will emphasize that he is only applying for a sales position with companies selling similar ranges of products to those he has sold previously, or those that you are marketing. If he has applied for a position with companies in varied fields –

consumer goods, capital equipment, services, he is not seeking a career, he is just looking for another job.

3 'If you were now the interviewer and I the salesman, what would you ask me as a final question?'

What you are now trying to discover is whether he possesses both common sense and mental agility. This is a very difficult question to answer on the spur of the moment. The answer I have usually received from men of ability is: 'Mr Johnson, there is only one final question I would want to put to you: I have made up my mind, have you made up yours?' Or 'My final question would be: when can you start?'

If the applicant lines up with your requirements, this should be your final query: 'Are there any other questions that you would like to ask me?'

Usually the strong applicant will say, 'No, you have explained everything admirably.' The weak applicant may reply, 'Can you tell me more about my holidays, or luncheon vouchers . . .?' This kind of answer could mean that your previous assessments may not have been right, and you will have to think again.

If the outstanding applicant replies that he has no queries, you should ask him: 'If, then, I offered you the job, would you accept it?' If the applicant answers 'yes', engage him, subject to references. Do not risk his attending other interviews after leaving you.

If, on the other hand, you are preparing a short list and you are still uncertain – if you wish to see other applicants before deciding – you will answer, 'I am delighted to hear it. I feel confident that you can be an asset to us but, as you know, there are other applicants whom I have to see today. By tomorrow morning I shall be able to prepare a short list. I feel confident that you will be on it and I shall telephone or write to you tomorrow, to let you know when we shall be meeting again.'

If the applicant answers, 'I should like a day or two to think it over', you will know that he has either applied for another position or you have not convinced him of the benefits of joining your company. You can either ask him which aspects of the job he wants to think about, or you can do as I usually do, and write that applicant off. There are exceptions to this rule, but they are very few.

The decision

It is possible at the end of interviewing that two, three, or four applicants, although having differing backgrounds and characteristics, are all suitable for the job. It is now that the essential and desirable factors in the main specification will help you to arrive at your decision. Whichever applicant has most of the essential qualifications should be given priority. If, however, two applicants have exactly the same essential qualifications, then the person to engage is the one whom the interviewer likes best – the one he would prefer to have as an associate.

PERSONAL HISTORY FORM
Confidential

All information given will be treated in confidence. No enquiries will be made of past or present employers without your prior consent.

In your own interest, please answer all the questions carefully. Where supporting evidence is normally issued, e.g. Scholastic or Technical certificates, this will be required for production at your interview with us.

PERSONAL DATA

SURNAME (block capitals) ....

Christian or Forenames ....

Address ....

....

....

Telephone No.: Private .... Business (Can you be contacted here?) ....

Nature of Residence (i.e. own house, flat, etc.) ....

....

Will you reside anywhere in the country? ....

Which areas do you prefer? ....

Does your company provide a car? ....

Do you own a car? .... Have you a current clean driving licence? ....

Date of Birth .... Age .... Place of Birth ....

Nationality: ....

Height ....feet..............................inches   Weight............................stone.....................pounds

Marital Status:...

Number and Ages of Children..

....

Have you any physical disability? ....

Details of any illness during the last 10 years which has kept you away from work for more than 14 consecutive days.

....

....

EDUCATION AND TRAINING

Please list in chronological order, Schools, Colleges, Universities and other places of education and training whose courses you have attended since the age of 11.

EDUCATION

| NAME and LOCATION | DATES | | EXAMINATION RESULTS |
	From	To	(state subjects)

FURTHER TRAINING (including Technical and Professional)

| NAME and LOCATION | DATES | | DETAILS |
	From	To	Include Diplomas, Certificates and other qualifications awarded. State whether full-time, part-time or correspondence.

FOREIGN LANGUAGES   (State proficiency in both speaking and writing)

LEISURE AND INTERESTS

Which publications do you read regularly? ....

How do you spend your leisure time? ....

....

Membership of Clubs, Institutes or Societies (indicate any office held) ....

Period of notice required if you were offered this appointment ....

BUSINESS RECORD

Please list in detail, in reverse chronological order, starting with your present or last appointment.

NAME and ADDRESS OF EMPLOYER	BUSINESS OF EMPLOYER	From Month and Year	To Month and Year	JOB TITLE	DUTIES	BASIC SALARY		OTHER EMOLUMENTS	REASONS FOR LEAVING
						At Start	At End		

PRESENT OR LAST EMPLOYMENT

1. What is the title of the person to whom you are responsible?

2. Give a précis of your job specification.

3. State the number of internal/external staff you control.

4. What do you consider to be the strongest part of your character?

5. What do you consider to be the area in which *you* would like to be trained?

6. What aspects of your job do you enjoy most?

7. What aspects of your job do you enjoy least?

ADDITIONAL INFORMATION

Please write about yourself here, giving any information which may be helpful in considering your application – for example, what are your long-term plans, your strong points, what affects your attitude to certain types of work and what influenced you to make this application.

Date ....   Signature ....

3 Motivating people to care
Alfred Tack

It is not possible for a company to inaugurate a customer-care policy unless care for its own people is given priority. No one will strive beyond the call of duty to satisfy customer needs when he, or she, feels that management is not caring for its own people. Newcomers to an organization do not arrive with love in their hearts for the company's customers; they have to be motivated to appreciate that their jobs, and the company's future, can depend on maintaining customer loyalty. Customer care is not a one-off project. It is the commitment of everyone, all the time, to provide a high standard of customer service.

There are many proven ways in which employees can be motivated to give of their best all the time, but motivation can only be effective if the salary structure is right. Let's face it, most people believe they are underpaid; and most people decide whether or not they are justified in their beliefs by comparing their rewards with those of others doing similar work. However, to ensure that all forms of motivation succeed, top management should regularly review the pay structure – by checking with one of the several salary surveys published each year, seeking advice from the CBI or the BIM, or studying situations vacant advertisements.

When checking such advertisements, remember that those inserted by employment agencies are not reliable guides. Often such advertisements are inserted to attract prospective employees, who must then register on their books. The advertisements to study are those where the advertiser is also the employer.

The pay structure should be fair, which means that in the main it will be acceptable. It also results in employees being motivated by means other than pay. What, then, will motivate a reasonably satisfied workforce to play its part in the company's customer-caring policy?

Setting an example

All employees are motivated when managers and the chief executive set the right examples. When the managing director in a company not doing too well decides to increase his own earnings by a large sum, while instigating a cost-cutting exercise, employees will not accept a 'work harder', or 'customer-care' policy.

When a manager regularly takes extra time off for lunch, why should the members of his team not take time off for shopping? This may result in a customer not receiving delivery of his goods on time, or not receiving a rapid response to a letter or telephone call. When a manager is ill-mannered and brusque to the point of rudeness, why should they be thoughtful and caring for people?

When a manager is upset on receiving a complaint from a customer and hurriedly dictates a 'get lost' letter, he cannot expect his secretary, who takes down this letter, to look with favour upon a customer-care policy. She will undoubtedly spread the news of the way the boss tackles difficult customers, and many of her colleagues will think that it's a good policy – far better than the customer-care one.

If a manager arrives late at the office and leaves early for whatever reason, he cannot expect good timekeeping from his subordinates, and without good timekeeping it is impossible to keep work up to date for the benefit of customers.

To carry out a successful customer-care policy the manager must set the right example in every aspect of that policy. It must be emphasized by the manager, over and over again, that the company's future always depends on the loyalty of its customers – and that loyalty is only won by better quality and better service.

Enthusiasm

The old tag runs: 'There's nothing so catching as enthusiasm – except the lack of it!'

So it is with customer care. Explaining to employees the policy and the benefits of the policy in a matter of fact manner, as if the manager is bored stiff with the whole idea, must lead to its failure. The policy will only succeed if the manager is enthusiastic about it, and shows his enthusiasm. If he tries to inspire others to try harder, so that everyone enjoys playing their part and all talk with pride to their friends and associates about how their company really does care for its customers, then success is assured.

Again, this enthusiasm can only develop if it begins with the chief executive. It is of little use sending a memorandum from the main board, setting out logically and clearly the company's objectives of giving greater customer care. The memo should follow a meeting where the managing director himself enthusiastically expounds his views to the main board, and should show the board's enthusiasm for putting the customer first and how it applies to the whole workforce.

Enthusiasm for customer care ensures a winning policy, one well summed up by Sir Colin Marshall, chief executive of British Airways, who said, 'Good managers must be totally willing to commit themselves emotionally. Traditionally, in Britain, we have considered it bad taste to allow ourselves to be seen to be emotionally enthusiastic when it comes to business areas. But emotional commitment helps other people to identify and participate, as well as giving them a good reason for associating with the concepts.'

Enthusiasm will always prevail.

It's important

In 1989 the middle-aged whiz-kids stopped whizzing. Men and women who had been upheld as the new society of entrepreneurs, whose deeds we were forever reading about in the newspapers, were leaving or being sacked by the companies they had built. Success had turned to failure.

Eminent financial journalists put the blame not so much on the high interest rates as on ambitions. The entrepreneurs borrowed heavily, to buy company after company, but they didn't have the management skills to ensure the success of these ventures.

Why did they want to achieve so much so quickly? One of the reasons, which may account for some of the people, was that they wanted to feel so very important. They enjoyed the publicity: bankers would kowtow to them, villagers tip their forelocks, and the ordinary person wonder at their great achievements. In other words, they wanted to feel important.

So it is with many of us. We react favourably to those who make us feel important, and quickly lose interest if made to feel that our job is not very important to our company.

For example, some managers find it difficult to say to an office cleaner, 'It is so important for us to impress clients when they call, and they are impressed if the surroundings are right. They are not impressed with unhygienic surroundings. We could even lose a large order if a customer's mind is clouded by disturbing thoughts even before a meeting is held. So much depends on you; just think of that!' Of one thing you may be sure: that cleaner who has been made to feel so important will strive to do better.

The statement made by the manager is true. We often form immediate impressions, good or bad, on entering a waiting room or even an entrance hall.

Why do managers find it so difficult to believe these words? The answer is simple: no one ever tells them of their importance as managers of transport, stockrooms, sales offices, credit control departments, etc. Making people realize the importance of the work they do is related directly and indirectly to customer care. When they feel important, they will be motivated to strive harder, knowing that their work is so worthwhile.

There has to be a constant reminder that every single job in a factory, shop, or office, has some bearing on customer care. This of course applies especially to retailing. Most shops and stores sell similar merchandise – few have monopolies in any one best-selling product. Why, then, should a customer prefer one shop to another?

The answer is good service. Sadly this service to customers is lacking in so many retail shops and stores. Why? Because assistants are not reminded continually of their importance to the company's welfare.

The greatest motivator

In some companies the workforce is motivated by threats. Fear may be a strong driving force, but it is not an acceptable motivator. In Germany it is workforce discipline that ensures a concentrated effort, but that can only apply to those countries whose people enjoy being disciplined – who thrive on discipline, and work happily under regulation. But in every country in the world people give of their best when their efforts are appreciated, and this applies to chairmen of companies, managing directors, managers, and right down the line.

When a City editor writes well of the achievements of a chairman, you may be sure that the newspaper cutting will be a cherished possession of that executive. He delights in showing the cutting to his family and friends, and such chief executives will strive even harder to achieve even greater results, to win more appreciation and praise.

When a manager is praised for some achievement, he walks on air for days, and will certainly not fall below his high standards, since appreciation and justifiable praise are the greatest of all motivators. Although so often stressed by psychologists and others interested in the field of motivation and human relations, appreciation is too rarely shown.

When I have lectured on this subject, invariably someone who prides himself on his toughness and bluntness will say, 'I don't agree. People are paid to give of their best, and if they don't they should either be kicked up the backside or kicked out. There is no room for sloppy sentimentality in business,' or words to that effect.

Then again, at a meeting someone will invariably say, 'I agree with your conclusions, but how do you separate flattery from praise?' And there is usually a hum of agreement at that from the other members of the audience.

None of us wishes to become a member of a 'flattery brigade', but that misconception can easily be dealt with. Flattery is either an obvious exaggeration or a lie. We all know when we honestly deserve praise – when we have done a good job.

The only time flattery is at all acceptable is when an after-dinner speaker who has been dreadfully boring is praised by the chairman for a wonderful, inspiring speech. Everyone knows that it is a lie, but the speaker himself cannot be insulted by being told the truth, since he has volunteered to give his services as an after-dinner speaker. So the chairman invariably congratulates this speaker on his excellent performance. All humbug! But the chairman has no other course.

The rule in business for all of us to remember therefore is that appreciation must be deserved, and praise should only be given when deserved. All of us strive to do better when we know that our achievements have been recognized, and we are told that we have done well. Unfortunately many chief executives find it difficult to praise anyone, and that characteristic is catching by others in management.

Think about yourself for a moment. When you take that new brochure you have designed in to your managing director and ask for his opinion, do you really want that opinion? Think carefully! If you are honest with yourself, you will know that what you really are seeking is his praise. If you receive it, you will be so happy; you will be flourishing that brochure in the faces of your colleagues at every conceivable opportunity – the boss thought it outstanding!

Another example: when you have satisfied, even delighted, that very difficult customer, how do you react when your manager says to you, 'That was brilliant! You sent him away a happy customer, not an ex-customer! I wish everyone could do that!' What do you think? Flattery? Of course not! It was the truth, and you will try to maintain that standard for ever after.

You are a receptionist on the switchboard, overworked, and under some strain, answering yet another call in the standard manner of greeting. Then you hear the well-known voice of your managing director. He says, 'That was a perfect greeting, Mrs Wright – congratulations, and many thanks.'

Suddenly stress disappears, frustration evaporates, and you smile with pleasure. Your day has been made!

We all feel better for honest appreciation and justifiable praise, and are more readily motivated to take better care of customers.

Challenge

Most of us feel better for accepting a challenge, especially if we are part of a team. Although this applies particularly to sport, it also applies very strongly to every aspect of business. You have been told, 'I don't think it's possible to send out a 10,000 mailing by Friday.' That is a challenge which somehow even the most cynical of employees will accept – if only to prove the boss wrong!

'It is asking a lot, I know, but with all your experience I believe you could get that repair finished by tomorrow,' is a challenge that, more often than not, will be accepted, and the engineers will strive for success. But although such challenges are highly acceptable, the one certain winner is the team challenge.

At the NuAire factory in Caerphilly we have instigated such a team challenge, which applies particularly to quality control. The results are flashed on a screen for all the workforce to see. The target obviously is *zero faults*. The challenge has been accepted, and everyone seems to enjoy the effort to improve the quality, and win a prize for their team. Such challenges do motivate the workforce.

Working conditions

Good working conditions do not motivate in themselves, although they do engender pride, and pride can be a motivator. But poor working conditions are certainly demotivators. It is very difficult to explain to some executives that badly kept lavatories, dripping taps, broken tiles, loose lavatory seats, and unemptied ashtrays, do not engender a good working spirit, and are therefore demotivators.

Too many bosses are apt to say, 'If we clean it up they won't appreciate it!' Our experience is that in the majority of cases good working conditions result in a better attitude, and less of the 'they don't care' syndrome.

The same applies to depressing factory and office areas, which could be brightened by a coat of paint or perhaps a picture on a wall.

It is rarely appreciated that poor working conditions are

a demotivator, and demotivation means that no one cares very much about looking after customers. A customer-care programme should include regular checks on employee facilities, and general decorations.

Status

Achieving, or having the objective of achieving, status is a motivator. It applies to almost everyone, in every walk of life.

This of course is linked with a career development programme and should apply to everyone, because nearly everyone likes to think they are capable of moving up a step or two and achieving status in the form of promotion. Most people are motivated to try harder if they are aware of a definite development programme, if they know that, provided they do well and outshine others by their work effort, or perhaps by producing original ideas, they will achieve another step up the ladder.

It need only be a very small step – it doesn't matter. Even the smallest step is one which enables a person to go home and tell his family that he has made it. Developing a career development programme is a motivating winner.

Incentives

Prizes, vouchers, free holidays, are all essential motivators for those concerned directly with selling, but rarely to employees in general. But one incentive that is a winning motivator is awards for suggestions for improvement in production or service – and of course customer care.

Motivating and customer care

Looking after customers does not come naturally; people have to be motivated all the time to give of their best. The chief executive should remind himself continually that when the going is tough, the difference between loss and profit can be the attention given to customer care. If the market is not growing, to keep profits moving upwards means taking business away from competitors.

When all things are equal – and so often these days there isn't a great deal of difference between products and prices, whether the product is a detergent dishwasher or price for price car – the business will go to the company that has respect for customer care – the manner in which it handles complaints, the care taken to ensure that deliveries are made on time, etc.

Whatever the economic problems of the country, a company whose workforce is 100 per cent committed to customer care – whose chief executive continually motivates managers in the ways set out in this chapter, and whose managers, in turn, motivate their subordinates – is the company that will prosper in spite of downturns or political changes. Customer care is all about motivating everyone to strive that little bit harder to give a better service.

4 Training for customer care
Alfred Tack

There can be all the willingness in the world by everyone to participate wholeheartedly in a customer-care policy – they may have been motivated to strive harder for perfection – but lack of customer care can stem not from being unwilling to consider the customers' needs, but from lack of skills or the knowledge necessary for the satisfactory completion of a task.

If a stock controller is baffled by a new computer system, but doesn't like to show his ignorance, a customer could wait 4 weeks or more for a delivery which has been promised in 2 weeks. If an accounts department manager sends out a short 'unless' letter to a customer whose account is not overdue, the reason could be a clerk's inability to keep records up to date. Unfortunately so many minor complaints or problems related to customer care are hidden from chief executives. When therefore they claim that 'My company really cares', they are not being untruthful; they just don't know what goes on in the various departments of their organization.

There is one way in which every chief executive can ensure that his company does care, and he need not fear that mistakes are being hidden from him. This is by instigating a training policy, or if one is already in existence, by ensuring that it is 100 per cent efficient. With a well-trained, highly motivated staff, the chief executive need have little fear of losing customers through employee inadequacies.

Setting up a training division

The first essential is to have a highly efficient person in charge. He is the training manager, although he may have other titles within the organization.

In the small company this could be the managing director himself, but medium and large companies should have a full-time training manager. He has to be qualified to originate courses for all employees – such courses to include management training. The success of a training policy depends almost entirely on the ability of the training manager. He, or she, has to be respected for specific qualifications, which could be in the marketing or the financial area. He should also be able to set up a plan for one-to-one training, to be carried out by supervisors, departmental managers, or even other members of the staff.

But let us first consider the holding of courses rather than one-to-one training. A course may be for three or four people, or for twenty or more; the number doesn't matter. However, the course content does.

The courses don't have to be held in elaborately decorated conference rooms, designed specifically for training. Any spare room that is available may be used. This is very different from outside training courses, charging fees. Then the delegate expects something in keeping with the fee charged and the reputation of the training organization. The reason I am emphasizing that any reasonable room in an office or factory is suitable is because I have been told so often by managing directors, 'Yes, we'd like to set up some form of training, but we haven't the space available.'

The next question is where do you find a highly competent training manager? It isn't easy, but never accept second best.

There are three ways: to advertise, to employ an outside personnel selection organization, or to use a manager already in the employ of your company. You'd be surprised at the number of managers who will enthusiastically develop the techniques needed to become good trainers.

Instructing doesn't come naturally. The art of holding the interest of a listener has to be acquired. When a training manager has been selected, no matter how experienced he is, he should be sent to an outside training the trainer course.

When judging such an applicant, ensure that he or she is a very good administrator. The training will fail if the administration is bad. A training manager must be able to lead from the front – to show others what to do by the examples he sets. If he cannot do this, he will not be acceptable.

Here is a checklist a managing director can use when selecting a trainer:

1 Knowledge of subject to be taught.
2 Enthusiasm for teaching.
3 An audible and pleasant voice.
4 A good vocabulary.
5 A logical thinker.
6 Sincerity.
7 Confidence.
8 Ability to lead discussion groups and workshops.
9 Willingness always to be available to give advice and guidance to others – to be a good counsellor.

Once appointed, his first job will be to confer with all managers to decide on training needs and priorities. Each manager should carry out an analysis to highlight the strengths and weaknesses of those employed in his department. The following questions should be asked:

(a) Is the telephone always answered before it has rung more than five times?
(b) Is there ever a part shortage? If so, extra training must be given in the stockroom procedures.
(c) How many letters are returned for retyping?

(d) Are there any personality clashes?
(e) Are there too many irrelevant print-outs from the computer?
(f) How efficient is the buying policy?
(g) Is training in production skills adequate?

Most salesmen undergo some form of training, but too often it is concerned mostly with product knowledge rather than selling skills. This should be changed so that there is more emphasis on the ability to close orders. In addition, an analysis of the sales division might show that there are weaknesses due to salesmen avoiding calling back on difficult customers. Salesmen must be taught that they are in the front line for customer care, and that it is their job to see that every customer is a satisfied customer.

Following the needs analysis, the objectives for the training courses can be set.

Training and Enterprise Councils

At the time of writing, all employers can seek the help of training and enterprise councils. When planning the incorporation of a training campaign, you will find that TECs can be most helpful.

One-to-one training

Usually a departmental manager delegates one-to-one training to a subordinate. A telephone receptionist would train a new recruit; a secretary may initially train typists in the general nature of the work; a garage hand may guide an engineer; a bank clerk keep an eye on the beginner at the next till; and so on. Provided guidelines are given and those who undertake the task of training have themselves been trained, the staff training will be a success.

Often the star salesman is the one directed to train

newcomers, and what does he do? He attempts to train them in his own image; but maybe that image cannot be copied. He may have a style of his own – one not generally adaptable to other people.

One of the surest ways to fail is to allow unsuitable untrained people, uninterested people, or even reluctant people, to train others.

The most likely person to handle training is a supervisor, but has he the time available to train others? If he or she is under pressure, the training may well be undertaken but it will certainly take second place to other routine tasks.

The only way to teach beginners is step by step. Never attempt to teach a whole concept in perhaps a 1-hour session.

With a telephonist/receptionist, for example, on the assumption that the quality of her voice has been checked at the interview, the first step will obviously be the job specification, so that the newcomer will know exactly what is expected, and the trainer will know his objectives. Next, the newcomer must gain a complete company departmental knowledge, coupled with the names of executives and those most often likely to receive telephone calls. The receptionist will be given a printed list, but will strive to memorize the names of those to be contacted when an incoming call is received. A regular study of the list will automatically bring this about. Speed of response is all-important to the telephonist/receptionist.

Often, when telephoning even a well-known and efficient company, the response is 'Hold on', and the 'hold' goes on for ever. Then, when contact is finally made, the wrong person is found to be at the other end of the line.

Recently, I wanted to make enquires about certain aspects of a car telephone. I was actually put through to seven different people before finally making the right contact. This general knowledge factor is so often overlooked by supervisors giving training. However, if there are many departments to cover, even this step should be broken down into perhaps four stages, rather than attempting to overload the mind of the new receptionist by asking her to memorize some fifty or sixty functions. No further training should be given until these first few steps have been mastered, and this may take several days.

The next step is for the receptionist to acquire a full understanding of the switchboard, if it is new to him or her. Again there should be no advance from this step until the supervisor is satisfied that the new receptionist's reactions to whatever signalling system is used are instantaneous. When the supervisor is confident that the receptionist is able to handle the switchboard effectively, then a check should be made as to the trainee's skills as a telephone receptionist. During the first 4 weeks there should be continual monitoring by the supervisor.

There can be as many as twenty steps in teaching someone to become a highly efficient telephone reception-ist, including method of greeting, handling difficult customers, keeping calm, etc. If possible, always allow the trainee to practise what has been learned, step by step, before progressing.

Underlying the training must always be confidence-building. The supervisor must never be anyone who is even slightly antagonistic towards the employers, other-wise the newcomer is likely to be hearing such statements as, 'Oh, you musn't take any notice of him!' or 'She does go on a bit, doesn't she? Just do it your way.'

The newcomer needs to know that he or she is working for a first-class, caring organization, and that the job is of importance. If there is a machine to be used – a typewriter, computer, duplicator, or photocopier – the trainer must ensure that before any training begins, that machine is operating satisfactorily. If this check has not been made, often the training will be ruined because of the time taken to rectify the machine, which may sap the operator's confidence.

Another aspect of one-to-one training is that the newcomer's personality and character should be evaluated while the training is taking place. Is he, or she, the nervous type, a quick learner, bombastic, aggressive, perhaps a knowall? Instant decisions must not be made, because sometimes these characteristics only show up under stress, and there is always stress in a learning situation. A trainee may agree that a task is fully understood, which may not be true. It may be that he or she feels that it is a sign of weakness to admit 'I still don't understand.' Anyone who has tried to use a word processor for the first time by studying the training manual will know the difficulties, and will also know how easy it is to tell a supervisor, 'Yes, I understand' when in fact there is no understanding.

If a clerical worker is to be trained, there should be some examination to ensure that the person understands all the forms that have to be completed, reports annotated, and procedures carried out. Again, the trainer must never ridicule forms, no matter how much he may dislike them. Saying, 'You needn't bother too much about this one' will lead to the trainee not bothering at all.

In the retail trade one-to-one training is essential, even though the company may operate a standard indoctrination course. The newcomer to a cash till, for example, does need the trainer by his or her side. Most of us at some time have arrived at a cash till to be met with the cashier ringing a bell to attract the attention of a manager. She doesn't know perhaps how to complete a transaction, or how to fill out a credit card form.

Of course the problem is always the time factor. In a busy office or factory no one ever seems to be able to find the time to help others. In a busy shop, assistants can become annoyed when asked by a newcomer for advice.

Advice, however, should never have to be sought, if the training is effective. In a department run by a highly efficient manager time will always be found for training. If staff cannot be available for such training, then the

manager himself must carry out the task. Staff training is a
number one priority if there is to be customer satisfaction.

All those who train, whether from a platform, sitting
beside a newcomer in office, shop, or factory, or
overlooking the work of a mechanic, must ask themselves
the question: 'Am I going too fast to enable this
newcomer to retain the knowledge?' The emphasis must
be on slowing things down. Probably the worst feature of
gabblers is that they believe they are being understood,
and do not subsequently carry out tests. The secret of
successful training is to keep questioning the trainee, to
ensure that all the teaching messages are being understood; and in order to enhance these chances, the quality
of the voice, and the slowness of enunciation are roads to
success.

In addition, many trainers are too happy operating the
machines themselves, like fathers with the childrens' toys.
A trainer must give trainees continual opportunities to
prove to themselves that they understand the intricacies of
the machines.

So much success depends on the trainer's personality.
No trainer should ever be appointed on a one-to-one basis
if he is apt to shout, remonstrate, shrug his shoulders as if
to imply that the trainee is a moron, or look appealingly at
a colleague, conveying the impression that the task is far
beyond the capabilities of the trainee to grasp. The word
for all trainers to remember, whether they be on a
platform or supervising in a shop, office or factory, is
patience. Without patience there can never be successful
training.

Trainees also need encouragement – something that
they don't sometimes receive, because the wrong person
has been appointed to train them. A trainer must always
make the trainee feel that he belongs to the department,
division, area, or shop, so that he is able to play his part in
its success.

There is one aspect of training often neglected, and that
is jargon. In every organization, and especially in the

electronic, engineering, or scientific field, there is trade jargon – words which are used continually, and which should be readily understood by any newcomer.

Typical of this would be the typist, who has to type from a recording on which the manager has indulged in one of his favourite pastimes – using the technical phrases he knows well, to bamboozle anyone who may not be so well informed. A list of such jargon should therefore be provided for the newcomer, showing the meaning alongside each word, phrase, or sentence.

Throughout the session the need for asking questions is essential, to make sure that the trainee has understood the point or points being made. Asking closed questions should be avoided. The *open question technique* is far more useful. For example:

- Tell me how you operate the plus and minus keys.
- Would you like to explain the techniques we use for sending out reminders when payments are due?
- What is the procedure for follow-up letters after enquiries?
- Explain how you would remove the binding.

The following is a checklist for one-to-one training:

1 Prepare carefully.
2 Always put the trainee at ease.
3 Explain how the trainee's task is a part of the whole company plan.
4 Explain the importance of the task.
5 Go carefully through the job specification with the trainee, and agree each point.
6 Teach section by section, step by step.
7 Talk slowly.
8 Emphasize all the key points.
9 Prepare an information sheet relating to trade jargon.
10 Build up the trainee's confidence in the company.
11 Ask questions continually – open questions wherever possible.

12 Ensure that all the equipment to be used is in order.
13 Be patient.
14 Never show boredom.
15 Keep giving praise and encouragement, and this includes talking about opportunities for advancement open to the trainee.
16 Make certain the trainee reaches a high standard of performance; then, for the first week or so, make continual checks, rather than wait for the mistakes to be made. The phrase 'Not bad for a beginner' is not good enough. It doesn't motivate.
17 Show appreciation of the work being carried out by the trainee when he or she is obviously trying very hard.
18 Allow the trainee to learn by *doing* rather than listening, although listening will obviously be important before there can be any action.
19 A most important factor is to ensure that the subordinate is trained in the task of one-to-one training. This of course applies to all forms of training and is covered in the next chapter.

To summarize

Martin Skan has been named Hotelier of the Year by his fellow hoteliers. He opened the Chewton Glen Hotel in Hampshire 25 years ago and turned it into one of the finest country hotels in Europe. Chewton Glen has won top awards for food, service and decor. From all over Europe and the States customers queue up to get into the hotel. Such is fame – also a great success story.

Recently Martin said, 'Anyone can build fancy places with bricks and mortar, but it is the staff who determine whether a hotel is excellent or merely good. If staff selection, training and motivation are carried out properly staff will themselves make sure of customer care.' To which some readers might comment that is fair enough for a hotel, but not nearly so simple for businesses.

The following is an extract from an article headed 'Fit to Manage', published in *Management Today* and written by Tom Farmer, chairman and chief executive of Kwik Fit and companion of the BIM.

> As a specialist, I set out to satisfy a customer need that had been created by the very industry of which we and other fast-fit operators rapidly became an important part. My customers needed no appointment, and my behaviour with customers was part of my individual ethic. As the business grew, I knew that I could never expect my colleagues to be nicer to our customers than I was to them. Now we operate personnel programmes which are based on respect for the individual, and which cater for his or her financial aspirations and career development. In addition to the pay package, working people need motivation, in which training and effective communication are highly important aspects. I had in any case always practised what management theory now calls 'MBWA' – management by walking about. It's obvious that personal communication is cheap and efficient, and gives feedback. Nowadays, it is supplemented by a massive investment in continuous training, in information technology, a specialised incentive scheme. The most important person is the customer, and it must be the aim of us all to give 100 per cent customer satisfaction, 100 per cent of the time.

These two comments sum up what the first four chapters in this book are about, selection, training and motivation, all three essential for customer care.

5 Training the trainer
Iain Cowie FCCA

Associate Director, TACK Training International Ltd

What are the attributes that enable a sales trainer to hold the attention of his audience and to be a well above average trainer. A survey carried out with delegates attending courses shows that the basic attributes, placed in order of importance, were:

- Knowledge.
- Enthusiasm.
- Audible and pleasant voice.
- Fluency.
- A good vocabulary.
- A logical mind.
- Sincerity.
- A sense of humour.
- Confidence.
- Empathy.
- Acceptable appearance.
- Ability to lead and control discussions.

This list provides a yardstick against which potential trainers may be measured. It also enables decisions to be made as to the areas in which the trainer should be trained. Let us consider these attributes in more detail.

Attributes needed by trainer

Knowledge

A trainer does not have to visit every country in the world to enable him to teach geography, nor does he have to be an astronaut to teach astronomy, but he does have to have a very full knowledge of the subject he is teaching.

Enthusiasm

The enthusiasts can never learn enough about training techniques. Enthusiasm being contagious, his love of his work, his obvious desire to help others, his vitality, will result in everyone attending his courses capturing his enthusiasm.

Audible and pleasant voice, fluency and vocabulary

These attributes are linked because they form the basis of good communication, and if a trainer cannot communicate effectively, he cannot teach. Weaknesses to look for are:

1 A thin voice, which cannot be heard clearly from the back of the room or lecture hall.
2 A monotonous or depressing voice – no change of pace, no tonal qualities.
3 A lack of fluency, which will result in many 'umms' and 'ahhs', and unnecessary breaks while the brain tries to recollect the exact word for the occasion.
4 A vocabulary so limited that the trainer is continually searching for words or else he uses several words where one or two would suffice.

A logical mind

The advantage of a logical mind is that it enables the trainer to present each facet of a session in an understandable and logical sequence. As none of us can be certain whether we are logical or not, it is perhaps safer to believe that we are not, and therefore to take greater care in preparing and rehearsing sessions, finally seeking outside advice as to whether or not the session does present a logical case.

Sincerity

If a trainer talks with his tongue in his cheek, does not really believe in his own teachings, and is mostly concerned with his own aggrandizement, he will be unable to disguise his insincerity, however great his oratory or dynamic his manner.

Sense of humour

We all know that 'we' most definitely have a sense of humour, but as for that other fellow! Can we be objective about ourselves? We must try, if we want to succeed as a trainer, but a trainer should not attempt to tell funny stories, or try to be a comedian, to arouse interest. That is not good teaching.

A sense of humour really means being able to laugh at oneself, and being able to inculcate humour into our description of events, rather than telling a funny story, which, almost surely, is not new and which others will have heard before.

Confidence

The effectiveness of a trainer depends greatly on his self-confidence; confidence which enables him to win over the most difficult trainee; confidence to know that he will still give a fine session in spite of a splitting headache, or having had a row with his wife about money that morning. His confidence will be derived from knowing that he has studied his craft and worked hard at his location; that he will not lose his nerve if, temporarily, he forgets his lines or he discovers that the visual aids won't work.

That belief in himself, that confidence obtained from hours of hard work and study – particularly studying himself and his actions – will enable him to enjoy every minute of the session. And when a trainer enjoys the session, almost certainly the trainees will do so as well.

Empathy

The dictionary definition of empathy is *the power of entering into another's personality and imaginatively experiencing his experience.* Very simply, from a trainer's point of view it means being on the same wavelength as his audience.

Acceptable appearance

The rule for a trainer must be that nothing in his appearance should distract attention or detract from his performance. His dress and general appearance must be totally acceptable to all the trainees.

Ability to lead and control discussions

Discussion groups will inevitably fail unless the leader controls the discussion. This the trainer must be able to do, or he must be able to appoint someone else to be the leader, knowing that that person has the qualities necessary to control discussions. Never leave a group to work by themselves, without someone being in command to guide the discussion.

There are two additional attributes that could complete the make-up of the perfect trainer: platform manner and organizing ability.

Platform manner

Trainees can become restless – even annoyed – at a speaker's mannerisms. No one can concentrate for long on fine oratory when a trainer keeps walking about the platform waving his arms or constantly repeating a word, or a hackneyed phrase. He should only gesticulate when the movement is linked directly with a point he is making. For example, if it pertains to products to be sold worldwide he might circle his arms, and the connotation would be quite clear. But generally it is better to avoid arm and hand movements as much as possible.

There are many other mannerisms, including constantly playing with some object – a pen, a book, an ashtray, a tie, a handkerchief. It's all right to do anything once, but it is repetition which distracts the listener.

Organizing ability

It is a confidence loser when a trainer has to make excuses:

'I'm sorry, but the projector is not working.'
'The administrator forgot to put out the notes.'
'I must apologise but one of the magnetic aids is missing.'

A good trainer must also be a good organizer.

Instruction checklist

In addition to the attributes listed, a trainer can still fall short of complete effectiveness if he does not adhere to the nine golden rules of teaching:

1 Never stare at one or two of the trainees, to the exclusion of all others. Never let your eyes roam over the first two rows only. Those at the back of the room also want to be included and they are included if you *look* at them.
2 If possible, avoid asking an individual trainee a direct question. Frame the question so that it embraces the whole of the class, each one being unaware who will be chosen to answer it. If a trainer does not do this, as soon as one trainee is questioned, the rest of the class will relax, feeling *'that doesn't concern me!'*
3 If a trainee answers a question, or raises a point during question time, he will usually speak directly to the trainer. Those alongside or behind him often cannot hear what he is saying. The trainer should either invite the trainee to move away from his seat to enable him to address the class, or, more usually, the trainer will repeat the trainee's words to the class, before answering.
4 Trainees should be told to keep questions short, otherwise there may not be enough time for all the questions to be dealt with.
5 If a trainee raises a point, he must be allowed to complete it. He must not be interrupted or cut short, however often the point may have been raised at previous courses, or however irrelevant it may be.
6 No trainee should ever be made to look foolish. There must be no sarcastic remarks or unkind leg-pulling at the expense of a trainee. A trainer may denigrate himself, but not others.
7 A trainer should never make tactless remarks about a country, county, race, religion, or a political party.
8 No matter what the provocation, a trainer must never lose his temper with a trainee.
9 Use key sentences and confidence cards as memory aids.

Key sentences

How is a trainer to remember a session's total content? He can:

(a) Write it out fully and read it.
(b) Write it out fully and memorize it.
(c) Write it out fully and extract notes to which he can refer during the session.
(d) Write it out fully and memorize key sentences.

Write it out fully and read it

This is the certain way to bore everyone.

Write it out fully and memorize it

If a trainer has such a fine memory that he can memorize a session without any trouble, he is a fortunate person. But how many people could memorize six, seven, or eight sessions?

Write it out fully and extract notes for reference during the session

This the normal procedure, and it can work reasonably well, provided the notes are legible and can be immediately understood by the speaker. Unfortunately many trainers write notes that are too long, or there are too many of them, necessitating constant study during the session. Although they were quite clear when the session was being prepared, they become a frustrating jumble of words when the trainer is actually on his feet, speaking.

Write it out fully and memorize key sentences

A *lead-in* sentence is the best memory aid of all.

How to evolve key sentences

First write out the session in full; then extract all key points – the six or eight steps which form the main teaching objective of the session. Now underline the main sentence that lead in to each of these points. Polish up the sentences so that they clearly indicate the area to be covered during the next few minutes. Remember, they are *reminder* sentences.

The answer – confidence cards

Why cards?

Cards are easy to handle and turn over. They do not become crumpled. They can be held together by a ring, if necessary. All TACK trainers, however experienced, however many times they have given a session, never go on to a platform without their confidence cards.

The cards should be approximately 12 cm × 7 cm – the size of a postcard – and each divided into three sections. In the top left-hand section write the main sentence. Use the right-hand space for exhibits or visual aids. Across the

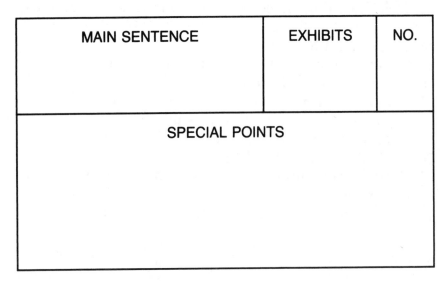

Figure 5.1 *Confidence card*

bottom write special points to remember. Number each card in the top corner of the right-hand section.

The cards are illustrated in Figure 5.1.

Confidence cards really do give a trainer the confidence of knowing that no important fact will be omitted from a session, and that he cannot possibly lose his place or dry up.

Having chosen a person who has a good chance of becoming a skilled trainer, the manager must consider the skills and knowledge required, to be able to produce and present effective courses.

Techniques for instruction

The skills required are those which enable the trainer to help others learn, and may be summarized as the ability to:

1 Identify training needs in the organization.
2 Identify necessary changes in knowledge, skills and attitudes.
3 Write learning objectives for courses and individual sessions.
4 Understand how people learn.
5 Select training strategies that will aid learning.
6 Create a balanced training programme.
7 Choose appropriate and varied training methods.
8 Create course notes and case studies.
9 Be able to use training aids.
10 Build rapport with trainees.
11 Deliver the training capably, and make the experiences enjoyable.
12 Assess the learning achieved during the training session.

These show the procedures to be adopted in training the trainer to create and run a training scheme. They each deserve further examination.

Identifying training needs

The training needs of an organization arise in two ways.

First, there may be specific *corporate* training needs that arise from a change in the business enterprise itself, perhaps after a takeover or when there is to be a fundamental change in the way the business itself is done. This may be due to changes in technology, computerization, or when the directors feel that an attitude change is required, such as a commitment to customer care, quality or safety.

Second, there may be specific *individual* needs for certain knowledge, skills and attitudes in order to equip employees for their present or impending tasks.

The identification of corporate training needs is primarily the responsibility of the board of directors of a company. The identification of individual training needs is more complex. In order to do this task properly, we must get line managers to produce job specifications for each task within the organization.

The key tasks to be undertaken in each job should be identified in the job specification and each key task split into task elements. Each element may then be analysed in terms of the knowledge, skills and attitudes required to perform the job effectively. A job profile may then be produced for each job, showing the requirements of the job in terms of knowledge, skills and attitudes. Each identified requirement should be given a weighting, as shown in Figure 5.2 (p. 70).

Identify necessary changes in knowledge, skills and attitudes

As a second step, each employee should be profiled against the same list, first by the manager and then by the employee. The line manager and employee should then discuss and agree the individual profile and then compare

JOB: Trainer

Scale

0   no knowledge/skill or poor attitude

to

5   full possession of knowledge/skill or good attitude

Knowledge	Requirement
Product	3
Process	3
Professional	5
Leadership skills	
Motivation	5
Communication	5
Counselling	4
Management skills	
Organizing	5
Measurement	4
Procedures	5
Safety	4
Motor skills	
Trade	1
Computer	4
Telephone	4
Driving	5
Attitudes	
Loyalty	5
Self-discipline	5
Quality	5
Safety	5

Figure 5.2 *Job profile*

it with the job profile. When the job specification demands a 5 and the employee performing the job rates an agreed 3, there would seem to be a training need. On the other hand, it may reveal that the employee possesses qualities that are being under-utilized by the firm. Perhaps these qualities should be recognized and the employee moved to a post where he or she can be better used.

A continuous assessment system should then be set up, requiring line managers to make a point of meeting with each subordinate at, say, 6-monthly intervals. At these meetings they should discuss progress and set targets for the following period. This gives an opportunity to discuss, among other things, the areas which present difficulties to the employee and specific individual training needs. It would be wrong, however, to consider these occasions as the *only* time this subject should be raised. An open atmosphere should be fostered, so that the employee feels able to communicate training needs to the line manager at any time.

Write learning objectives

This is perhaps the most difficult task for a new trainer – and indeed for the more experienced trainer. A new trainer should first of all focus on the fact that these are not teaching objectives but *learning* objectives. They must be written in a form that emphasizes the change in knowledge, skills and attitudes as a result of training. The objectives will be written first at a course level, then at a more detailed session level.

Understand how people learn

The human brain is capable of storing all experiences perceived in a lifetime yet using only a very small part of its available capacity.

People are most open to learning when they want to learn and when they enjoy the experience. Not everyone will have good memories of school, but they may be helped to become open to learning by a good trainer.

High intellect is not a prerequisite to learning. More important is an interest in the subject, high motivation and the intention to recall material. An intelligent person who is low on these will learn very little, while a relatively unintelligent person may learn very much more, given interest, motivation and intention to recall.

Delegates may be motivated by being told what they can expect to achieve as a result of their efforts. This statement of benefits should be expressed early in each session in terms such as 'at the end of this session you will be able to . . .' This puts the emphasis on the pay-off for the individual and motivates far better than 'I'm going to tell you about . . .', which focuses on the trainer rather than the trainee.

Select training strategies that will aid learning

Given the session objectives, the trainer should be able to identify the key points – those which must be achieved in order to achieve the session objectives. For each of these a learning strategy must be devised. While academics may identify six different levels of learning relating to educational objectives, for practical purposes we may relate easily to three: reflection, understanding, and memory.

Memory-level learning

Objective: that the trainee knows the date of the signing of the Magna Carta.

For this, learning at memory level only is required, and we need a strategy that fixes the relation between the Magna Carta signing and 1215. Some trainers will use repetition, some will review repeatedly, and others will use a mnemonic such as 'It's quarter past twelve (12.15), let's sign the Magna Carta!' It may be silly but it works. In fact the sillier the mnemonic, the better it seems to work.

Understanding-level learning

If the objective is to create understanding, or long-term memory, then a different strategy may help.

Objective: to recall the stopping distances shown in the highway code to enable the trainee to remember these long after the driving test has been passed.

Few drivers will remember these for long, as they use memory-level learning only. They adopt the strategy of repetition until they recall the few examples given. If they are to be recalled some years later, understanding-level learning will be more appropriate.

It is possible to derive them from a simple relationship which may be easily remembered. See Table 5.1.

Table 5.1 Stopping distances

Speed (mph)	Thinking (feet)	Stopping (feet)	Total (feet)
20	20	20	40
30	30	45	75
40	40	80	120
50	50	125	175

Key learning points:

(a) Thinking distance is the same as the speed in mph.
(b) Stopping distance is the speed multiplied by the speed divided by 20.

For example, take 70 mph:

Thinking distance	70 feet
Stopping distance 70 × 70/20	245 feet
Total	315 feet

Those who understand this relationship will not forget, although they may need some time for mental arithmetic.

Reflection-level learning

Effectively get the group to figure it out for themselves. This may be done by using methods such as:

1 Guided discovery (asking a series of questions leading to the discovery).
2 Group discussion.
3 Case study.
4 Business project.
5 Role play.

Where an objective is of vital importance, the trainee should consider using a reflection-level strategy. Where the objective is to change an attitude, the only way of achieving it will be by adopting a reflection-level strategy.

Use of various levels

Objective: that the trainees will give up smoking.
  You could try

(a) *Memory level*
    Repeat twenty times 'Smoking is bad for me'. Rather childish and likely to have the opposite effect from that intended!
(b) *Understanding level*
    A government health warning on every packet. Already tried that – it failed!
(c) *Reflection level*
    Discuss in a small group the pros and cons of smoking. Make a list of these in order to report back to the full group.

A change in the trainee's attitude can only be brought about by the trainee – such an approach helps the trainee to consider his or her attitude logically. Why else is group therapy found to be effective by Alcoholics Anonymous and in psychiatric care?

Used well, a reflection-learning strategy will also produce understanding and memory-level learning.

Create a balanced training programme

In considering a full day's training, the trainer should be aware of the limits of attention span and the external influences inhibiting learning. Attention levels will start high and then begin to drop as time goes on and the presenter relaxes. Towards the end of the session they will begin to rise again, as the trainer realizes that he or she is 'in the home straight' and gives signs of concluding.

In consequence a training session should be kept to a reasonable length to avoid loss of attention. Short breaks should be given between sessions to allow the following session to be started on a high. Delegates are usually happy to absorb input from the trainer in the morning but will require a bit more action and participation after lunch, particularly when lunch has been generous.

Evening work, if required, should be of the syndicate exercise or project type, with little trainer interference. Trainees need to take control of the situation occasionally. Few adults are happy to be directed day and night by another, however skilled the trainer may be.

Choose appropriate and varied training methods

The trainer has to be able to keep a sense of occasion during a course and keep the trainees' interest with a variety of training methods. Some of these will be highly controlled by the trainer, with little input from the trainee. At the other end of the extreme, the trainee may control the session while the trainer's role is to stand back and give the trainee the room needed to develop.

There are many different training methods in common use, the more obvious of which are the following.

Lecture (often known as chalk and talk!)

This is a one-way communication method which may be used for:

1 The presentation of facts.
2 An initial outline of a subject.
3 Presenting material not available from one source.
4 Provoking criticism.

Step by step presentation

Similar in style to the above, with one vital difference – feedback – making it a two-way communication technique. Understanding is tested as the topic is unfolded by well-planned questioning technique. Used for all the purposes shown above.

Step by step discussion (guided discovery)

Confined to asking questions which gently and unobtrusively lead the delegates through difficulties to the realization of the session's objective.

This method is one of the most useful (but time-consuming) methods available to us. Use it sparingly for critical points to:

1 Encourage the delegate to think.
2 Give pride of ownership in the discovery, which makes it unforgettable.
3 Obtain participation and thus enliven the proceedings.

Reading

A method which may be useful in certain circumstances but which seems a poor use of contact time to most. Use it between learning sessions to:

1 Obtain knowledge and information.

2 Promote analytical and evaluative thinking (if coupled with a report back to the group).

Programmed learning

This method uses a series of 'frames' down the left-hand side of a page on which a little reading is followed by a question to which a response is required. The answer is to be found on the right-hand side of the page – one frame lower than the question.

The idea is that the learner should cover the page with a sheet of paper so that the response may be determined before sliding the paper down to check the answer on the right; then he continues to the next frame on the left.

Such a programme is time-consuming to write but easy to use again and again, once available. It may be used:

1 Where immediate feedback is required.
2 Where lessons are to be given to one or two.
3 To pass on knowledge and information.
4 To deal with simple problem–solving.

Demonstration

Performance of an operation that shows a phenomenon or skill, while the delegates watch with the objective of performing the task themselves later.

This method will be useful to:

1 Help delegates to learn by observation.
2 Gain a knowledge of principles.
3 Encourage participation by the introvert.
4 Allow interchange of ideas.
5 Encourage use of, and familiarity with, technical language.
6 Gain feedback.
7 Allow delegates to express findings in precise terms.

Directed discussion

A number of small groups are given a topic to discuss, a clear objective and a short time allocation in which to achieve it.

This method is useful as part of a session for:

1 Collection of facts.
2 Testing understanding through interchange of ideas and opinions.
3 Encouraging the delegate to think.
4 Engendering participation and giving variety to the session.

Open discussion (buzz groups)

Groups of two to six members are asked to discuss a problem for a short period within a session.

This method may be used to:

1 Encourage participation by the introvert.
2 Allow interchange of ideas.
3 Encourage use of, and familiarity with, technical language.
4 Gain feedback in discussion.
5 Consolidate learning by 'rehearsal'.
6 Encourage group cohesion.
7 Encourage delegates to express their findings in precise terms.

Free group discussion

This is a learning situation in which both the topic and the objectives are set by the delegates. The 'teacher' merely observes the session.

The purposes of such a session are to:

1 Observe changes in power, attitudes, feelings and communication between group members.

2 Encourage delegates to listen and be open to other people's ideas.
3 Make the delegate aware of his/her attitudes and communication style.

Case studies

Any method giving an opportunity to apply theory to realistic everyday practical problems will come under this heading.
Used for:

1 The practical application of learning.
2 Encouraging the delegate to analyse and evaluate data.
3 Encouraging the delegate to recognize interrelations between items of data and consider their significance.
4 Providing insight into the nature of decision-making.

Brainstorming

A spontaneous discussion, during which participants are asked to suspend their critical faculties in order that ideas are not stifled. A ridiculous idea may lead to a solution by expanding the thinking of the group.
This method may be used to:

1 Encourage creativity.
2 Allow interchange of ideas.
3 Encourage tolerance and listening to the ideas of others.
4 Allow mature and thoughtful consideration to be given to the topic.
5 Gain feedback by requiring delegates to express their findings in precise terms.
6 Reduce barriers to changes in attitude.

Synetics

This is a development of brainstorming, in which a mix of group members from different disciplines are asked to produce a creative solution to a problem. In addition to the above-mentioned objectives, this will make participants aware of the possibilities of problem-solving by 'bouncing ideas off' colleagues in different departments. You may be familiar with the idea of 'quality circles', one popular application of synetics.

Problem-centred groups

Similar in many ways to small group discussions, but the group may extend from four to twelve members discussing a task, and the time frame may be longer.
This is useful for:

1 Extending the powers of analytical and evaluative thinking.
2 Decision-making.
3 Applying the principles discussed in an earlier session.
4 Changing attitudes within the group.

Syndicate method

The class is divided into groups of around six members, working on set problems, with intermittent help from the trainer and reporting to the group on their work.
This method may engender an element of healthy competition and may be used:

1 To encourage effective group management.
2 To add impact by self-tuition with the group.
3 To acquire skills in seeking and organizing information.

Seminar

An essay or other work is presented and used as an introduction to group discussion.
This method may be used to:

1 Encourage critical thinking.
2 Engender thinking.

3 Give individuals the opportunity to present an argument in front of other influential experts.

Individual or group tutorial

A session devoted to a single student or a small group. It may be used to:

1 Gain feedback and clear misunderstandings.
2 Encourage and develop an introverted student.
3 Develop and drive thinking deeper into a subject.

Individual task

This may consist of a problem to work out in a class or a series of practical tasks, each performed by one individual.
The method may be used to:

1 Encourage participation.
2 Make learning an active process.
3 Deal with problem-solving.

Projects

These may be devised to give a fair degree of freedom to the learner while remaining carefully structured and controlled by the presenter. This method may require a great deal of time, and is perhaps better used between learning sessions rather than during them.
This method will help the delegate to acquire knowledge of how to:

1 Seek and obtain relevant information.
2 Organize information.
3 Present information.

Practical sessions

This method may be used in many forms, but normally requires a submission on paper reflecting the practical skills or knowledge gained as a result of the project.

May be used to:

1 Develop ability to seek, organize, apply and illustrate knowledge and skills.
2 Refine presentation skills.

Short presentation by delegate

Capable delegates are asked to conduct research between group contact periods and report back to the group.
This method may:

1 Encourage mature and thoughtful consideration of a topic.
2 Develop insight by forcing the delegate deeper into the topic.
3 Develop the delegate's abilities to gather and structure relevant information.
4 Improve the delegate's presentation and persuasive abilities.

Audio tapes

Tape recordings may be played to a class or to individuals. This method may only be used in short bursts, as the other senses (particularly sight) tend to distract from hearing.
This method may be used to:

1 Illustrate the importance of the voice.
2 Illustrate telephone technique.
3 Provide variety.
4 Promote self-awareness.
5 Demonstrate social interaction.

Tape/slide sequence

This method adds visuals to the audiotape method described above, and may be used when a standard message must be put across to a group of people dispersed by time or geography. It is more than just audio plus photographs and, if done well (some systems use up to 16 projectors under computer control), can result in an absolutely stunning show at a fraction of the cost of a similar videotape.

May be used to:

1 Communicate visual information.
2 Train small groups or individuals at a time convenient to them.
3 Communicate a standard message.

Video or film presentation

Pre-recorded training films and videos may be used:

1 To present information.
2 To bring the outside world into the training room.
3 To develop or change attitudes.
4 To present situations and personal reactions for consideration as case studies.

Close circuit recording and playback of delegates' performance may also be valuable to:

1 Enable objective self-assessment to be made.
2 Review reactions and consider how they could have been improved.
3 Open delegates' minds to attitude changes.

Video recording by delegates

Delegates are set the task of producing a short video on a topic relevant to the course, e.g. a TV advertisement on a marketing course.

Valuable to:

1 Clarify and concentrate thinking.
2 Aid creativity.

3 Add impact to a message.
4 Develop teamwork.
5 Work to deadlines.
6 Develop role play.

Role play

When personal or inter-personal skills are called into play in a training session, role play will almost always prove useful, although perhaps time-consuming. It must be handled carefully, to avoid embarrassment.

The technique may be used to:

1 Enable a delegate to use new insights in an interactive situation.
2 Enable a delegate to make errors in an open and accepting environment.
3 Encourage good listening while trying to achieve one's own objective.
4 Encourage behavioural changes by proving the effectiveness of a technique in action.

Computer-assisted learning and computer-based training

The term computer-assisted learning is normally applied to situations where the use of the computer is incidental to the training, whereas computer-based training generally refers to a learning experience under the control of the computer. The computer's main advantage is its ability to be programmed to recognize responses and give immediate feedback.

The computer programming need not be difficult, but the writing of the material to be programmed may be quite difficult.

The technique is best used to:

1 Deal with one learner at a time, where short periods may be available.

2 Teach the workings of the computer and programs (standard spelling).
3 Make the learner respond to set questions.
4 Analyse the responses made and report at the close of the session.
5 Measure the effectiveness of the learning.
6 Provide a printed record of the accuracy of responses given.

Simulation and games

A simulation is a representation of reality that may be physical, abstract or mathematical. A game is played when one or more players compete for pay-offs according to an agreed set of rules. A simulation game combines these features.

Such techniques may be used to:

1 Produce positive attitudes towards a subject.
2 Gain active involvement.
3 Provide experience similar to the real world.
4 Emphasize the structure of the relationships in the model.
5 Demonstrate the relevance of knowledge.
6 Experiment in a safe situation.

Action mazes

An action maze is a book in which you read the first few pages, which set a scene; then you are forced to make a decision, on the basis of which you will be instructed to pass to a page number that appears to have been randomly selected. You will then be given further information, which builds on the decision you made, and further decisions will pass you backwards and forwards through the book until, finally, you emerge from the maze, having perhaps taken several wrong 'turns' in the meantime.

This technique may be used to:

1 Show the results of poor decisions.
2 Illustrate the most effective means of achieving an objective.
3 Give opportunities to correct a poor decision.
4 Reinforce key learning points.

Interactive video

This system requires a computer and a video disc system. The principle is that you watch a short video recording that gives a scenario and requests you to make a response to a question. Your response, which may be one of around four or five possibilities, is fed to the computer, which is programmed to prompt the video to show you the next piece of action, based on your response. A program may require some twenty responses. In principle it is an action maze without the need to turn pages or read.

Note that it is possible to use video tape rather than disc, but the access time in selecting the precise piece of tape required may by unacceptable.

Training instruments (personality profiling)

This method refers to questionnaires that may be used to gain some ideas of the attitudes of the individual towards work and people. They may prove revealing to the individual who has responded to a series of questions that are set in everyday situations and help him/her to be aware of attitudes that may have become part of his/her general outlook on life.

They should be used to:

1 Reveal personal attitudes.
2 Open discussion as to desirability of ingrained attitudes and opinions.
3 Lead towards reassessment of attitudes and beliefs.
4 Open the individual to suggestions of possible behavioural changes.

Create course notes and case studies

Different firms will wish to adopt different house styles for their training notes, but as far as the trainee is concerned they must be:

1 Well-indexed.
2 Brief while encompassing all key points.
3 Illustrated by relevant examples.

Writing a case study or project is a much more difficult task than might appear. It is necessary to give sufficient information to provide context, key facts and clear instructions as to the requirements of the task.

Be able to use training aids

However good the presenter, a delegate on a training course needs more than the sound of a voice to direct and command attention. An experienced trainer will be aware of the effect of body language and positioning within a room on the delegate – how moving forward will add impact to what is being said and moving backwards will diminish it.

While the face and body comprise the most interesting and responsive visual aid, many other media can give visual and aural impact to a presentation. The other senses – feeling, smell and taste – are more rarely used in a training situation, but can be of advantage when appropriate to the objectives. Many training aids are available. The presenter should be able to use them blindfolded.

The flip chart

The most commonly available training aid can be used as a large notepad visible to a larger group. Because it is so easy to use, however, it is often abused.

Some thought should be given to the use of the flip chart in advance of a presentation and it should not be used just on the spur of the moment. It has the following advantages:

1 Pre-prepared visuals may be built up and revealed.
2 Reference back is easy.
3 The use of bold colour can add impact.

Use it as follows:

(a) Keep the presentation simple.
(b) Keep writing level.
(c) Write only in block letters.
(d) Check for width before writing.
(e) Keep it level.
(f) If spelling is a problem, you are standing too close; step back and check before continuing.
(g) Pencil or yellow crayon guidelines will not be seen by your audience. You can pre-prepare a stunning visual for drawing live.
(h) Flip over as soon as you finish using the board – it may retain their interest when you are moving on.

Magnetic white board

This has most of the advantages of the flip chart without wasting paper, but you have to spend time rubbing out your work.

The advantage of magnetism is the ability to place pre-prepared, colourful, plastic magnetic shapes, with words embossed in different colours, which stand out clearly. These shapes may be moved around to illustrate points. This saves time in writing, ensures legibility and, if pre-checked, covers spelling difficulties.

The overhead projector

One of the most useful means of transmitting pictures to the brain of the delegate, the overhead projector is more often used to transmit words!

In choosing an overhead projector you should consider:

(a) Portability.
(b) Robust construction.
(c) Second bulb with switch-over control.
(d) Quiet operation of the fan.
(e) Good throw of light.

Avoid the models with a mirror base and the lamp in the head – as the slide heats, it may expand and present a double image on screen. It also reduces the number of overlays you may use as light must penetrate them twice.

Competence in the use of this equipment is crucial to the confidence of a presenter. Poor use is very noticeable, while good use may add considerably to a presentation.

The following are tips for professional use:

1 Check the equipment before use:
   (a) Plugged in?
   (b) Switched on?
   (c) Bulb (and spare) live?
2 Tilt the screen to avoid the 'Keystone' effect (verticals converging as they drop).
3 Use an acetate roller over the lens, for:
   (a) It prevents the amateur writing directly on to the lens;
   (b) you may write on the acetate, then roll on.
4 Use stiff cardboard surround on slides, for it
   (a) aids positioning on the projector;
   (b) gives a crisp edge to the visual.
5 Get slides in order (number them consecutively).
6 Have two slides made up rather than search for one for re-use.
7 Know where you will store the slides, before and after use.
8 Know where to stand when displaying a slide (by the side of the screen).
9 Design your slide so that you can distinguish all important elements from this position (if you can't, neither can your delegates from the back of the room).

10 Use 'revelation' technique when you wish to focus attention. Reveal the slide by moving a lightweight but dense masking paper (with no punch holes) that has been placed under the slide. The reason for placing the mask *under* rather than *over* the slide will become apparent when you only wish to cover the bottom inch of your slide!

11 Alternatively, where new information is spread over the area of the slide, the use of 'overlays' may provide impact. Limit the number of overlays, as the light penetration will drop with each additional sheet.

   The actual number of overlays you can use will vary with the type of acetate used. Try it and see what is acceptable.

12 Be careful in your selection of colours. Some colours do not transmit well on screen, although they may look stunning on the artwork.

The 35 mm projector

For some presentations 35 mm projection may be preferable to overhead projection. This medium must, however, be used with extreme caution.

The advantages of this medium include:

1 A clear, bright image.
2 Quick-change facility.
3 Good magnification of detail.
4 No obstructions to viewing when the projector is correctly placed behind the audience.
5 Slides may be easily produced with equipment and skills which are generally available. It must be said, however, that the skills are less available than the equipment.

Against these advantages, we should consider:

(a) The need for dimming of lighting.
(b) Ease of damage to equipment.

(c) The image takes attention from the presenter.
(d) Loss of eye contact with audience.
(e) The fact that of eight ways of inserting slides in the magazine only one is right.

If this medium is to be employed, then:

1 Use a magazine (carousel), check it and seal it before use.
2 Put slides in glass mounts if for long-term use (this has a second advantage of preventing 'popping' – slides may expand with the heat of the bulb and pop out of focus).
3 Use an experienced projectionist.
4 Use a reliable remote control – preferably an infra-red wireless model.
5 Arrange help (and cues) for dimming if necessary.
6 Finish with a dummy slide to prevent blinding your audience by moving past the slides.
7 If possible, arrange rear projection on to a translucent screen to reduce the dimming required.

Computer projection

This is a medium that is developing quickly. Costs are coming down and quality is improving rapidly. The screen display on a personal computer may be transmitted to an LCD projection panel placed directly on the overhead projector, and the image is projected as normal. Monochrome or colour may be used, though the latter is more expensive.

Alternatively, but even more expensively, the computer may be linked to a video projector to give a full colour visual image.

This technique has great potential, limited only by imagination and technical ability to control the computer. It will have increasing utility as individuals master its use.

The cine projector

Not used as often as it used to be, owing to the advent of the video recorder, it will give a very large image and potentially good sound, bringing the outside world into the training room.

It can, however, be cumbersome and noisy, requires professional operation and lacks flexibility. The potential for breakdown and running repair under pressure is high. For this reason most presenters prefer video.

Video television and projection

Many individuals now possess video recording and playback equipment, and have confidence in the reliability of the equipment and their ability to control it. They may not, however, be aware that there are several video tape and TV standards around the world.

It is necessary to check first whether the tape is VHS, Betamax or U-matic (which is quarter of an inch wider), and if it matches the video player in use. Then one must check whether the recording is made in the PAL (British), SECAM (European) or NTSC (North American) standards. Triple-standard video players are available, but they must be matched by triple-standard TV monitors. This is not a full list of systems and standards, but covers those in common use.

A 25-inch monitor may be sufficient for viewing by up to 25 people. Two monitors may be placed to deal with 50. For greater numbers, video projection may be necessary. This requires extensive focusing to get a good quality picture, and may suffer from a drop in quality as you move toward the side of a room and away from a direct viewing angle, although newer projectors suffer less from this technical problem.

Visual aid design

What looks good on paper does not always look good on a large screen.

In designing visual aids you should:

1 Keep them simple.
2 Limit the use of the lower third of your slide.
3 Prefer landscape to portrait format.
4 Use dark colours for impact.
5 Do not over-use colour.
6 Do not clutter the visual with irrelevant material.
7 Prefer graphs or charts to text or numbers.
8 Consider the use of cartoons.
9 Remember TEXT is NOT VISUAL.

If you insist on using TEXT then:

(a) Limit yourself to a maximum of *seven* lines of text per transparency.
(b) Limit it to *six* words per line.
(c) Justify your text left or centred and use larger fonts for titles.

TITLES
Sub-Titles
Text

(d) Your smallest print should be as large as the word TITLES shown above, i.e. use 8 mm and larger.
(e) Use bullet points (●).
(f) Leave a clear margin of 2 cm all around the frame.

It is vital that the author should try it out on a colleague and an average trainee. Only by doing a dry run can he/she ensure that the material written is complete and as clear as was intended. The author may not have committed to paper some fundamental point which was in his or her mind. The difficulty is to balance full information with the need for clarity and brevity.

Build rapport with trainees

A good trainer is able to reduce tension in a training situation quickly and make trainees feel that they can drop their ego-defences and make mistakes in an open and accepting environment.

The attitude of a trainer towards the trainees will come over in body language, the choice of words and the inflection in speech. It is at its clearest when asking or responding to questions. Thus good questioning techniques are critical to an effective trainer.

Questions may be used during a training session for many different purposes:

 1 To get and maintain interest.
 2 To open up discussion.
 3 To keep trainees alert.
 4 To direct the discussion.
 5 To stimulate and guide thinking.
 6 To bring in quieter trainees.
 7 To get trainees to think for themselves.
 8 To measure retention.
 9 To check understanding.
10 To determine student attitudes.

Trainers should be required to sit in a session as delegates periodically, to remind themselves of the horrid feeling in the pit of the stomach when a trainer directs a poor or inappropriate question at them. Good rapport is built as the members of the group begin to feel confident that the trainer is not going to embarrass them. They will then begin to relax and learn.

Questions, manner, body language and voice must all be non-threatening. The first question will set the scene so it must be good – prepare it beforehand.

A good question is purposeful, clear, and concise; limited to one idea; challenging; and clearly related to the objective.

It may be addressed to the whole group. Give them a few seconds to think, then ask for a volunteer. Scan the group for body language – direct eye contact says, 'I have an answer and am confident enough to give it,' head down says, 'Please don't ask me.' Your eye contact and encouraging smile may be enough to persuade a brave one to volunteer. If no one does, then smile, relax, and ask a more confident delegate by name for an answer. If you have read the body language well, there will be no further problems. Respond encouragingly to the answer, and congratulate the giver if merited. Once the initial resistance (if any) is broken, follow up quickly by passing a supplementary question around the group, bringing others into the discussion. Once they see you welcome and encourage contributions from the trainees, they will relax and participate.

When they ask you questions, listen carefully. The temptation is to start preparing the answer while the question is being asked. If you do, you may well answer the question you thought the trainee was going to ask, and not the question actually asked.

Rescue the trainee who asks a silly question, or one perceived as silly by the other trainees. Realize that they are being difficult. You will then gain the respect of all the trainees, who may think, 'There, but for the grace of God, go I.'

Your responses to trainees' questions will provide the best barometer of their attitude towards you. There are a few potentially difficult delegates on training courses. Some do not realize that they are being difficult. Others may deliberately be setting out to bait the trainer. In each case the trainer must ask himself why they are behaving in this way before he selects the best way of resolving potential conflict.

Some of the more common types who create difficulties for the trainer are listed below, along with possible responses:

1 The over-talkative delegate may be:
(a) Naturally verbose.

  (b) Well-informed, and keen to show it.
  (c) Wanting to show off.
  (d) Trying to be helpful.

  Allow the group to discuss his ideas. Ask a difficult question to slow him down.

2 The argumentative delegate may be:
  (a) Upset by personal or job problems.
  (b) A professional heckler.
  (c) Genuinely in disagreement.

  Listen and try to find merit in a point. Keep your temper firmly in check. Other ways are to pass points to the group, or speak to him privately.

3 The bored delegate may be:
  (a) Demonstrating superior knowledge (genuinely or mistakenly).
  (b) Demonstrating superior status.
  (c) Lacking in motivation.
  (d) On the wrong course.

  Check his knowledge by asking his opinion. Indicate respect for experience/status (only once, or the group will resent it). Speak to him privately.

4 The timid delegate may be:
  (a) Naturally quiet.
  (b) New to the subject.
  (c) Sensitive.

  Compliment him the first time he talks sincerely. Protect him from embarrassment; check his understanding; don't push him.

5 The delegate who always asks for advice may be genuinely trying to get the best out of the course, using you as a consultant. Ask the group whether the question is relevant to them. If so, give an answer. If not, defer it to a private meeting.

Deliver the training capably

The skills needed in delivering a training session are many and diverse. Good presentation skills are necessary, whether dealing on a one-to-one basis or presenting to a small group. These skills may only be gained by practice and constructive feedback from competent professional presenters who are respected by the trainee.

Note that feedback is given, not criticism, highlighting strengths and points for improvement, not weaknesses. The trainee should view a video of his or her presentation immediately after the review. Some feedback may not have been accepted by the trainee, but, on viewing the video, the trainee will better understand why the feedback was given and will accept the points made.

Assess the learning achieved during the training session

Most trainers will agree that assessment of learning achieved during a training session is difficult.

Evaluation forms are not objective, and may not contain the real thoughts of the trainee, who may believe the trainer would be hurt or become smug if he recorded his true feelings.

A more objective assessment may be gained through feedback obtained from a third party, preferably after the trainee has had an opportunity to put the training received into effect in practice. The only real alternative to this is by the use of the examination technique known as 'objective testing'.

The objective testing method is not as might be thought a method of testing objectives, but is rather a method of testing that is objective in itself. This objectivity is ensured by the fact that the questions and the marking scheme are all agreed before the test is taken. The marking then contains no element of subjectivity.

The technique relies on the use of multiple choice

questions to check the retention, understanding and reflective abilities of trainees.

Questions, known as 'ITEMS', have three parts:

1 A 'STEM', which poses the problem.
2 A 'KEY', which is the one totally correct answer.
3 'DISTRACTORS' – incorrect but plausible alternative answers.

Example of objective testing

A typical simple item is shown below:

According to UK market research, the percentage of dissatisfied customers who will not complain *and* not come back is:

(a) 96 per cent.
(b) 80 per cent.
(c) 20 per cent.
(d) 64 per cent.

The STEM of this question is the first sentence, 'According to UK market research, the percentage of dissatisfied customers who will not complain and will not come back is:'.

The KEY is answer (b) 80 per cent.

The DISTRACTORS are not all randomly chosen. They have been chosen as plausible alternatives because:

1 96 per cent is the percentage of dissatisfied customers who will not complain. Some of them may, however, come back.
2 20 per cent is the percentage who do not complain but who tell more than ten others of their dissatisfaction.
3 64 per cent is a randomly chosen but plausible alternative.

This last distractor is usually the most difficult to compose. Most trainees will approach such a question by trying to eliminate the most unlikely answer, thus increasing their chances to one in three instead of one in four. In this question such an approach is unlikely to eliminate the 64 per cent answer.

No more than ten to twenty questions should be given, and the exercise should be introduced as a 'retention exercise' rather than an 'examination'. It is used to judge the effectiveness of training techniques, and not the quality of trainees.

Conclusion

Having considered the knowledge, skills and attitudes required of an effective trainer, we may see clearly that the job of 'telling the others', given to an inexperienced member of staff, is clearly very difficult. With no prior experience or training, no one can be realistically expected to teach, motivate, and enthuse staff in training.

6 Performance appraisal and customer care
Philip Bourne MA

Director, TACK Training International Ltd

The objective of any performance appraisal scheme must be to *improve* the performance of the whole organization. As caring for the customer is a crucial ingredient in achieving good performance, the scheme must recognize this, and include practical means to cater for it. There are reasons why performance appraisal schemes do not always win the respect or approval of managers and managed: some are unwieldy, requiring masses of paperwork, the relevance of which is questionable; some are mere box-ticking exercises. In other cases weak managers have used them as an excuse not to manage on a day to day basis. 'I'll leave that correction until the appraisal – it's only 3 months away!' Even more frequently, schemes have been viewed solely as vehicles for salary reviews, regrading, and merit rises.

Each of these reasons misses the fundamental fact that appraisal is about performance improvement and better customer care. But there are spin-off benefits: better communications; and the chance for subordinates to air their views, their identification of training needs, career path planning, discussion of development opportunities and the contribution of information to any performance-related pay scheme. But the main objective is general performance improvement.

The fundamentals of any good appraisal scheme are:

- The identification of job, and personal objectives.
- The clarification and conversion of these objectives into standards of performance.

- An assessment of actual performance against standards.
- Analysis of the reasons for any deviations.
- An interview between appraiser and appraisee.
- Resetting standards for the next review period.

In all these areas the concept of customer care will be important – none more so than in the primary step.

The need to identify and set objectives is recognized in all good organizations. At the heart of the plan will be the fundamental objectives of the organization. They will fall into the categories of economic, human and social objectives, with respective emphases on financially measurable criteria, people development and motivation, and the organization's image in all three categories. Objectives will be broken down into departmental and subsequently individual job objectives. There will be few of these that should not contain an element of customer care, especially if the total quality management concept is embraced by the organization.

Objectives should be clear signposts as to what is expected from people, but they will need to be clarified, explained, detailed, made measurable and specific. In this form they are usually described as standards of performance.

Standards of performance

When standards are set they require to be:

1 Agreed.
2 Realistic.
3 Valid.
4 Measurable.

Appraiser and appraisee should agree the appropriate standards of performance before they are put into operation. If the chief imposes a standard, there is a strong chance that the subordinate will demonstrate that it is not achievable. If the chief asks the subordinate to set his or her own standards, he/she may possibly volunteer to hit a level of performance far higher than is required, or even achievable. So both parties should be in agreement as to what is required.

Standards should be realistic, which means achievable even if challenging. To demand an ideal performance, such as 'No customer complaints in a year', would be very demotivating to a manager who had reduced complaints from 200 to 20 – apparent failure! This does not mean that we should not have ideals such as the elimination of all complaints; but in practical terms people work better towards what they believe they can achieve.

The validity of standards is one of the most important aspects of appraisal. 'Valid' means that it relates to the requirements of the job, and not to the whims of the manager. Clearly such standards as a 15 per cent conversion rate for a salesperson, 5 per cent machine downtime for a maintenance engineer, or half a per cent reject rate for a production supervisor, are absolutely valid. So, too, would be 'every telephone call to be answered before the fifth ring' for a company telephonist.

Making standards measurable will help with the assessment and analysis of performance. It will also be far easier to explain to people, and allow them to monitor themselves. Areas such as communication, supervision and administration can cause problems with measurability, but these are usually surmountable.

Attitude is an area of consummate importance in caring for the customer, but, again, it can be apparently hard to measure. What will be the effects of 'the wrong attitude'? No repeat business, increased complaints, more disputes about prices and delivery . . . All measurable factors.

Armed with agreed, realistic, valid, and measurable standards against which to perform, the subordinate will be able to assess his or her own progress thoughout the appraisal period. And so will the appraiser. There should be very few surprises at appraisal interviews!

Assessment

Assessment must be relevant, accurate, complete, and explicit. Any appraisal can bring the danger of straying away from the valid standards originally set, because of extraneous or emotional factors affecting the appraiser's mind. Thus relevance is of prime importance. Judgement is against the standards agreed, and nothing more. It can be a temptation to compare the individual's performance with other people's, rather than with the set standard, which is wrong. When the assessment shows a performance that is very close to the standard set, there will be little need to do any major homework before holding the appraisal interview. But when there are deviations, and the standard is considerably exceeded or, more usually, performance has fallen short, the vital step of analysis must take place in preparation for the interview.

Analysis of performance

Managers who are committed to customer care will be using the tool of analysis regularly. Even the least formal of appraisal schemes will be built around it. Analysing performance problems follows a number of well-defined steps through to identification of the source of the poor performance:

1 Description of the problem.
2 Evaluation of its importance.
3 Elimination of external factors.
4 Identification of its cause.
5 Planning the means to overcome it.

It is a fairly confident assertion that if you cannot write down what the problem is, you will be able neither to cure nor discuss it. Writing it down will show you what you will need to tell the subordinate, and in what terms. If you cannot write it down, then it is probable that the problem does not exist, and it is certain that you will not convince your subordinate that it does.

Let us take an example of an office manager who is concerned about the performance of two of her senior clerical staff. She is worried about Jane's attitude, and is offended by the untidy state of Derek's desk.

She finds little difficulty in writing down in graphic terms a description of Derek's desk. It is covered randomly by work papers, newspapers, magazines, samples, items of equipment, tapes, empty coffee cups, unidentified plastic containers . . . But it is far more difficult to do the same for the 'attitude' problem.

The question must, then, be asked: 'Does it really matter?' Does the behaviour, or problem, really affect the results that the person is supposed to deliver? Does Derek's untidy desk result in a failure to achieve the results he should be producing? Does Jane's different way of doing things adversely affect her results?

If Jane operates within budget, consistently reduces internal and external customer complaints, is respected and liked by colleagues and customers, and seems to be on course to achieve all set measurable standards, it is probable that it does not matter that she works differently from her boss. If any of the above fail, then it is likely that it does.

Derek's untidy desk will matter if he frequently mislays important papers because of it; if others cannot fathom his 'system'; if his example is followed by more junior staff, whose efficiency is impaired thereby; if the desk is a fire, or safety hazard; or if, most vitally for the cause of customer care, customers visit the office, see the desk, and are concerned at the lack of apparent order. They might, then, take their business elsewhere, and that certainly would matter! But if none of these factors applies, the untidiness quite possibly does not affect efficiency, it merely offends the boss's sensibilities.

If, then, we recognize that there is no real substance to our concern, we have to learn to live with it, preferably with good grace! But managers are human, and if the lady manager in our example becomes neurotic about Derek's desk despite its lack of real importance, she can, at least, appeal to his better nature. 'Look Derek, please do this just for me, eh?' This is where managers who have established sound moral authority may score.

Most times the problem will matter, and then it is important to move on to discovering its origin and nature. So a vital next question is, 'Are there any external constraints or factors that affect the performance?' Do matters completely outside the person's control govern the achieved performance, making it impossible, or very difficult, to achieve the required results?

Legislation, economic or demographic factors, natural disasters, unforeseeable changes, political shifts, are just some of the factors that can prevent performance being as good as expected. It is fair to take them into consideration. A salesman whose territory potential is diminished by the closure of a number of major customers; a production manager whose workforce is radically reduced by mass resignations following a health scare about one of the company's products; a site manager whose partly completed buildings are razed by an unseasonable hurricane – all might justifiably expect to avoid blame for things over which they had no influence.

Sometimes the appraiser will be able to do something about the constraints, especially if he or she has imposed, or permitted, them in the first place. More often it will be a question of altering standards, of working with and counselling the appraisee, to help him or her cope with the situation of restructuring or reorganization.

But where there are no external constraints on the individual performing as required, the next and most significant question must be asked. 'Is the failure due to lack of ability or willingness?' Sometimes there will be an element of both, but it is vital to identify the cause of the problem before attempting to cure or contain it. To throw incentives at an already highly motivated but unskilled worker is as surely to court disaster as to send a demotivated one to yet another training programme to relearn what is already well known.

If the analysis shows the problem to be one of lack of ability, further investigation is necessary. It may be that there is a skill shortage, or the job has grown more complex, requiring greater organizational skills. New technical aspects need understanding. In these cases the solution is comparatively simple: the provision of the most appropriate training, in order to instil the necessary new level of skill.

Maybe further investigation will disclose that the lack of ability is far more deep-seated. It may relate more to a personal quality deficiency that is not susceptible to improvement by training. Innate intelligence and its constituent aptitudes such as numeracy, logic, speed of thought, analytic strength, creativity, insight and foresight are generally set in a person's development. You will not easily train someone to be more creative than is in his or her nature. Training cannot change people's character or personality; the introvert will always be an introvert, even if you train him or her to practise good interpersonal skills.

Thus, when the ability deficiency is identified as one of personal quality, i.e. innate, the customer-care philosophy dictates that the decision must be whether to change the job or change the job-holder. If the deficiency is but a minor part of a job that is otherwise carried out to a high level of expertise, it may be correct to remove that aspect from the job, and replace it with something within the holder's competence. If it be more fundamental, then the holder must be transferred or dismissed.

It is logical that the answer to the inability versus unwillingness question should be considerably weighted towards unwillingness. If that were not the case, it would point to deficiencies in the organization's selection, promotion, and development programmes of worrying proportions. Psychologically, however, managers seem not to want to recognize that the vast (four to one) majority of performance problems stem from unwillingness or attitude. This is probably because problems in that category are largely the fault of the managers themselves.

People who can perform as required but don't are very rarely anarchists, militant activists, bloody-minded anti-establishmentarians, or psychological misfits. They are usually ordinary people who do not recognize that good performance is in their own personal interests. This indicts their managers, who do not show them that it is. The whole concept of customer care will be nullified in such cases, so it is of paramount importance that we address the problem.

Why does a reasonable, well-trained and qualified person's performance sink to unacceptable levels? One reason is that the boss of the company is seen to punish good performance. The 'willing horse' is overloaded with difficult jobs, whereas his uncooperative counterpart is lightly laden. The non-complainer is seen to get nowhere, the loyal servant to be overlooked, the tireless worker to be unrewarded, save by being given yet more work.

The corollary is of course that the boss is seen to reward bad performance. The person who does not achieve objectives is, nevertheless, promoted. The grumbler loses the unpleasant jobs, mistakes are rectified by others without comment, the boss who delegates takes the job back at the first sign of difficulty. Above all, no one says or does anything to correct the poor performance. It is forgiven, ignored, covered up.

If we are to care properly for all our customers, we must ensure that our people are only rewarded for good performance, and that there are real consequences to them personally for falling below the standards set.

It is fairly common failing in many organizations that people do not understand the reasons for performing to a given standard. The salesman who submits his reports with poor grace, little application, and often late, may not know that they represent a vital input to the marketing intelligence of his company. The engineer who delays his expense claim form may not understand that it contains data critical to costing, cashflow, and management information systems.

Communicating the reasons for performing to standard may be enough to prevent some people performing poorly.

After analysis comes the positive step of the appraisal interview.

Frequency of appraisal interviews

There is no universal answer to the question, 'At what frequency should appraisal interviews occur?' If annually, it may be seen to be part of the payment structure; also, once a year is quite a long interval for such an important part of people management. Shorter cycles have the disadvantages of consuming much managerial time, and possibly being taken less seriously. Six months is about right.

Whichever frequency is chosen, the interview should be looked upon by both parties as vitally important. No interruptions should be tolerated, and both parties should come together fully prepared to utilize the time to the greatest advantage. The assessment and analysis should be fully aired, with a view to resetting standards for the next period, based partly on experience gained from this one. The appraised must be allowed to raise any matters of concern that he or she may have about the job, the future, the company, other people, and, especially, customer care.

Pre-appraisal checklist

1 (a) Check the job specification. Be certain that the specification has not been changed.
  (b) Be certain that no directives issued can affect or influence the subordinate's work.

- (c) Check to make sure that there is no substantial difference between actual performance and standards set.
- (d) Make certain that standards have not been changed, in case they have been beyond the control of the subordinate.
- (e) Carefully analyse any differences between performance and standards set.
- (f) Have any problems that might have reduced performance arisen?
- (g) Re-read all notes from previous assessment sessions.
- 2 (a) If the subordinate hesitates, do not help him out – let him discover the truth for himself.
  - (b) Never jump to quick conclusions when arriving at your decisions at the end of the interview.
  - (c) Be certain that you understand the subordinate's answers or questions.
  - (d) To clarify matters, use such sentences as:
    - (i) 'Am I right in believing . . .?'
    - (ii) 'Tell me if I am wrong, but . . .'
    - (iii) 'Am I to assume that you don't believe that you . . .?'
  - (e) Work out a standard sequence in advance and check continually that you are keeping to that sequence and not being sidetracked.
  - (f) Allow him time to talk about his successes.
  - (g) Discover if further training could help him to reach higher standards.
  - (h) Ask the appraised to tell you how he believes his career is developing.
  - (i) Remind yourself continually that during the appraisal is not the time to discuss salaries, expenses, or even promotions. Communicating the reasons for performing to standard may be enough to prevent some people performing poorly.

After analysis comes the positive step of the appraisal interview.

The appraisal interview

Appraisal interviews differ from selection or disciplinary interviews principally because they should provide no cause for surprise, no new information, and no real show of formal authority. Here is a checklist of practical tips on running successful appraisal interviews:

1 Always give sufficient notice of the time of the interview, so that both parties may prepare thoroughly.
2 Ensure that there will be no interruptions, so select the most suitable venue.
3 Try to minimize formality. Sit around a coffee table rather than hold the interview across your desk. This will encourage the exchange of views.
4 Don't forget to praise good performance.
5 Make all criticism constructive.
6 As far as possible, discuss measurable facts.
7 Be on the lookout for signs of emotion. Body language may give you clues that the appraisee is angry, frightened, resentful, or euphoric.
8 Diffuse the emotional subject, or take a break to let it subside.
9 Use the skill of constructive listening. Strike an attentive posture; look at the appraisee virtually all the time; encourage him or her with nods and smiles.
10 Ask open questions to encourage complete answers. Avoid closed questions, unless you are establishing facts or getting final commitment. Use words and phrases such as 'tell me about . . .', 'explain how . . .', 'describe . . .'
11 Do not fall into the trap of asking a good open question, then qualifying, and possibly even nullifying, it by closing it down, e.g. 'Tell me about your relationship with the accounts department. Are you getting along any better now?'

12 Get commitments and ensure that the interview ends with an agreed action plan, usually in the shape of the completed appraisal form, with its new performance standards.

Notes

Some notes will be made during the appraisal, others at its conclusion. The following gives some indication of the type of notes that might be made:

(a) Note the subordinate's results over the past 6 months, compared with standards.

(b) What actions are needed to improve the standards?

(c) Did the subordinate seem lacking in enthusiasm, judgement, or common sense? No subordinate would admit to such weaknesses; it is up to the assessor to decide what action is to be taken to put things right before the next assessment.

(d) Note down the general appearance of the subordinate – manners, his opinion of colleagues, did he criticize them unnecessarily, or did he use the weaknesses of colleagues to excuse his lack of achieving standards?

(e) Note down the subordinate's views of the assessment itself, and company policy.

(f) Note down general impressions so that they can be checked at the next assessment. Was he argumentative? Did he lose his temper quickly? Did he seem to be a reasonable person? Did he complain about the way he was treated? These notes will enable the manager to decide what action is to be taken to help the subordinate to cure his problems before the next meeting.

(g) What specific improvements were suggested to be achieved by the next assessment date?

(h) Rate the subordinate in comparison with others. Rate him against his success or failure to achieve targets, general behaviour, etc.

Praise

Always remember at the conclusion of the interview to find some aspect of the subordinate's contribution for which appreciation can be expressed. While criticism should always be tempered by kindness, if praise can be given, it should be unstinted.

7 Quality customer care

Brian Moss OBE, BSc, CEng, FCIBSE

Chairman, NuAire Ltd

Organizations that care for customers satisfy the needs of those customers. Axiomatic maybe, but, more and more, *customer care* is an expression used specifically to describe the improving of human relationships at the immediate customer/company interface. While good *front-line* staff/customer relationships, and especially the ability to cope with difficulties and complaints, fall clearly under the heading of customer needs, they can only constitute part of the total meaning of the phrase. Organizations genuinely concerned about customer care must satisfy *all* their customers' expectations, and this means that they must aim *not to accommodate mistakes but to prevent them occurring*, to eliminate them at source. Any fudging of this principle will lead inevitably to failure, because, sooner or later, competition will get it right and no amount of *partial, or superficial, customer care* will hold customers who can obtain a better quality total package elsewhere. Customer care must be directed towards continuously improving the total quality of the organization.

Customer care demands that the intrinsic quality of the organization itself is improved. This is self-evident when the BSI definition of quality is considered: 'The totality of features and characteristics of a product or service that bear on its ability to satisfy stated or implied needs'. Although ponderous, this *official* definition nevertheless strikes a chord with the opening sentence of the chapter, when satisfying the needs of customers was identified as the criterion by which customer care must be judged; there can be no other.

It is important, at this early stage, to comprehend the concept of *quality* fully. In everyday speech quality is synonymous with excellence, whereas in the business sense it is a judgement of how well a product, or service, satisfies what is expected of it. Quality cannot be an absolute measurement, because different people have different needs, and even those needs change with time and circumstance. Good quality as far as one application is concerned may be bad quality for another. For example, a cooking utensil that is considered of good quality by a busy commercial chef may not be suitable for use in domestic or army field kitchens, where it will be too heavy, or too light, for the particular circumstances of the application.

Because industry, generally, defines what is required in terms of a specification, the definition of quality is often manipulated into *good quality is meeting the specification.* Thus, in the case of our ubiquitous kitchen utensil, the quality of the three products required to work in domestic, commercial and military kitchens depends on them satisfying quite different specifications, even though the function and form of the utensil are identical in each of the applications. This example brings out the critical importance of the specification reflecting accurately the true needs of the customer, and this is an observation to which we will return, time and time again!

Of course it is very easy to meet most specifications simply by exceeding the requirements, when it can be argued that the product, or service, because it will perform its intended purpose, is of good quality. However, I would argue that either the specification should have included a stated cost criterion, or that one was implied by the very nature of the application. In other words, I have gone back to the phrase used in the BSI definition: *the stated or implied needs of the customer?* Another way of laying this particular bogey is to modify the definition slightly to read: *good quality is exact fitness for intended purpose*. This definition leads us naturally, and in my view correctly, to regard excessive cost as the result of poor quality: unnecessary cost can always be attributed either to over-specifying or to exceeding the demands of the specification.

The great advantage of this interpretation is that it invalidates totally the objections of those whose philosophy is encapsulated in the wonderfully revealing question: 'Can we afford quality?' One would have thought that the success of the likes of Marks & Spencer, and, internationally, Germany and Japan would have now made the asking of that question a nonsense!

A book analysing the common characteristics exhibited by America's thirty most successful companies concludes that all of them are obsessed with quality. And the list of outstanding quality-based companies says it all. These successful companies, far from losing money, save money by good quality. That cannot be surprising when it is acknowledged that some 30 per cent of our time is spent correcting errors. This saving enables the companies concerned to invest more than they would otherwise have been able to afford in new product development, the finest equipment, better training – all to the customer's future benefit. And, remember, that by virtue of their good quality regime, these companies are already impressing their customers now. That is customer care!

Quality control and quality assurance

Quality is often associated with the words *control* and *assurance*. What do they mean and what is their relevance to customer care?

In very simple terms quality control is the generic term given to the procedures that enable a company to isolate non–conformance. In the manufacturing industries, where it was developed initially, it is a statistically based inspection regime that identifies faulty materials, faulty processes and, finally, faulty products, but the techniques are now being used more generally, and quality control is employed in every type of business.

Quality assurance, on the other hand, is directed towards preventing non-conformance, usually through the operation of clearly laid down and agreed systems and audits affecting all the departments engaged in the production process. Simplistically, quality control can be thought of as sorting the goats (non-conforming products) from the sheep (conforming products), while quality assurance prevents them mixing in the first place.

The UK is a world leader in the use of quality assurance, and the British Standard governing the technique, BS 5750, has been adopted internationally. Apart from the obvious fact that its use has improved the quality of British products, quality assurance has also introduced British managers to the critically important, but difficult to handle, concept of quality. In addition, quality assurance will also be a European Single Market requirement for certain groups of products.

Quality control and quality assurance rarely apply to the total business, including only those processes following the *market brief* and excluding those following the *initial completion* of the contract. From the point of view of customer care, this is a most unfortunate restriction, because many of the most important, and most difficult, areas of quality lie outside this sector.

Firstly, neither quality assurance nor quality control are concerned with any of the methodology prior to the *design* of a product or service. QA and QC therefore are not called into service while the company identifies market opportunities, carries out market research, drafts market appraisals, conducts feasibility studies, and plans projects; more importantly, they are not called upon in drawing up the most fundamental document in quality management: the brief of customers' needs. This document determines not only the critical specification of the company offer but also the service level requirements expected by the customer. Quality assurance and quality control have no input into the drafting of the criteria that will determine how the quality of the company should be judged.

Secondly, there is a similar lack of QA and QC following the initial completion of the project, because neither technique is employed, generally, to monitor after-sales service, customer experience and comment, and re-ordering patterns.

Both therefore are curiously isolated from the market place, a situation of no little irony, bearing in mind that the definition of quality is concerned only with the customer! It has led to the most persistent, and vociferous, criticism of the techniques – that although they may produce end products of admirable consistency, there is no guarantee that the products match the customers' requirements. For example, although the banks may have well employed QC and QA techniques to improve the quality of their service, neither would have told them something they later acknowledged, that their hours of business were not in line with those required by their clients.

Total quality management

It is primarily to overcome this objection that 'total quality management' has been introduced. It is concerned with all the processes of the business and takes, as its starting point, the definition and satisfying of customer needs. As such, it is synonymous with customer care; and nothing less comprehensive can accommodate the requirements set out in the beginning of this chapter.

Inevitably, as must be the case with any methodology that is so wide-ranging to encompass all the processes carried out in a business, total quality management draws on techniques proved to be useful. Therefore it employs the statistical analysis of quality control and the systems of quality assurance. In one critical respect, however, it is unique; and this is of particular relevance to customer care. The methodology succeeds primarily by concentrating on *defining and satisfying each employee's individual business needs*, on the understanding that internal improvement leads inexorably to an improvement in the external situation. In so doing, total quality management is recognizing publicly that company quality is the sum of the individual employees' qualities. It is scarcely an earthshaking philosophy, but it has initiated an extremely powerful technique.

It requires little extension of this thinking to appreciate another tenet of total quality management, that better quality cannot be imposed by management, but must be embraced voluntarily by employees. Management's role is to provide the environment that encourages a customer-caring, quality-orientated attitude. It can do little else, but invariably workforces respond positively to genuine encouragement by a senior management committed to a *consistently applied quality obsessive credo.*

Measurement is important, because it plots progress towards targets and provides the personal incentives needed by individuals contributing towards better quality. Everything worthwhile can be measured, but it requires experience to recognize those parameters that indicate genuine quality movement. Western management finds it difficult to accept that major improvement is often better built up from the aggregation of many small improvements, and, although it may be temperamentally difficult to resist, the grand scheme is usually best eschewed in the pursuit of better quality. The quality battle is won when everyone recognizes the worth of batteries of quality indicators all continuously improving.

The elements of a Total Quality Management programme are straightforward in essence. Their implementation is less easy, because management soon finds itself operating in strange waters; it cannot lead through command, it has to encourage somehow a grass-roots movement and, as if all that were not difficult enough, it has to reduce its bureaucratic role and communicate openly with the workforce!

But, firstly, it has to create a common company policy of aims statement with which everybody in the organization can identify. People need to understand clearly what the common target is and what it is that motivates the company, and they need to know in terms that can be adopted as their own. They want to work for a company that has high expectations, and one that raises their prospects. They respond to statements encapsulating a culture that lifts their horizons. If customer care and quality are about satisfying needs, then, quite clearly, the publication of the company's aims has to be a priority.

The statement is not easy to write, because it should set out, clearly and concisely, values and aspirations that are not usually articulated. And, while they must be inspirational and visionary, they must also be achievable, expressed in terms accessible to everyone, and seen to be genuine.

Clearly customer care will be given priority in the statement. For many, it may well be the first time they are introduced formally to the concept of satisfying customers, to how everything else is subordinate to that notion. *The development of a customer mentality has begun.*

In committing the company to quality improvement, the statement should confirm the company's responsibility for providing the appropriate management style, working environment, plant and equipment, etc., necessary for a quality improvement process to be successful. It will explain the crucial role of the workforce, stressing that everyone is responsible for quality improvement, that quality is an integral part of every employee's job.

This section may carry messages about improving communications within the organization and the envisaged pushing down of management responsibility. It should explain the effect of these changes in terms of the exciting future it holds out for all those working for the company.

Finally, the statement will probably confirm how the improvement programme will be a continuing process, because quality can always be improved. It will reinforce the message, explaining that constant improvement will be the target.

Here is an example of an aims statement published by Nu-Aire when it initiated total quality management in 1988.

THE ESSENTIALS FOR OUR SUCCESS

1 Meeting customer needs and expectations is fundamental.
2 People are the company's most important asset and will share in its prosperity.
3 Company-wide commitment to improving our quality is vital.
4 To develop a mutually beneficial relationship with our suppliers.
5 It is essential to demonstrate that quality is continually improving.

Earlier in the chapter, I referred to the fact that a feature unique to Total Quality Management is particularly relevant to customer care. *Total quality management works on the basis that everyone working in a company has a customer.*

By recognizing that all who do a job pass on the results of that work to somebody else (usually in the company), TQM is able to draw on extremely powerful forces to drive a company-wide quality improvement programme:

1 All employees are driven to improve the quality of their work by their customer, the person to whom they pass the results of their endeavours.
2 All employees, in their role of customer, compel improvement in the quality of the work being passed to them by their suppliers.

3 What quality is, and what it means to the eventual customer of the company, are emphasized constantly to everyone employed by the company.

By appreciating and developing the internal supplier/ customer relationship, total quality management releases huge resources of individual employee energy. Because of the intimate supply/receive/supply relationship imposed at every level of the organization, this total personnel energy is controlled personally. It is an arrangement that can produce heady results.

In practice of course management finds that considerable assistance is required when the notion is first introduced. Firstly, many employees, especially those engaged in routine office work, find it difficult to understand that *they* are suppliers and customers. Secondly, most employees, even when they come to appreciate, in general, that they depend on the work of those who come before them in a chain (their suppliers), while those who follow them (their customers) depend on their output, often find it difficult to recognize *their* own individual suppliers and customers. They tend, inevitably perhaps, to identify those to whom they are responsible as their customer, rather than those colleagues who depend on their output.

One way round this problem is to ask everybody whom they believe their suppliers and customers to be. When a chart is constructed, summarizing the results of this exercise, the loose, unmatched, ends of supplier/ customer relationships are then immediately obvious to those concerned, and people can see their positions in the grid.

In the market place we want to know what our customers want of us, what they think of what we supply, and how we can improve our performance. In other words, we want to improve our customer care! Exactly the same applies to our internal customers, the colleagues who work alongside us. We must ask them exactly the same questions. At the same time, our suppliers, again our colleagues but sitting upstream of the flow of work, will be asking us the same questions about their input into our own little internal business.

At this stage, there are a number of ways in which the situation can develop:

1 Staff discover that they are supplying what their internal customers need, but perhaps not in the manner, or to the timescale, wanted.
2 Exact identification of what it is that an internal customer wants may show that it differs from what the supplier had decided it was, or, more likely in a non-TQM company, what the supplier had been *told* it was, but that slightly modifying the output will bring about improvement.

   In cases such as these where no major change in the internal product specification is required, the situation calls for the parties concerned to agree what quality indicator(s) should be used to monitor progress and for these to be posted publicly on simple charts by the operators.

3 Internal customers, or suppliers, realize that their respective inputs and outputs cannot be reconciled without *major changes* to the product specifications and/or associated systems and procedures.
4 The company, through a *quality circle* (or quality team), may have identified that a certain area of the organization requires special investigation.

In these latter examples the procedure is to charge the appropriate quality circle with the task of recommending what should be done. The final composition of a quality circle must depend on the nature of the problem being tackled, but the general rule is that membership is drawn from as near *operator level* as possible, is *multi-functional,* and often includes representatives of *internal customers and suppliers*. Although quality circles are permanent, it is advantageous to change their membership regularly. Circles report to a quality management committee, which is responsible for the coordination of their efforts. Quality circles should always be charged with completing a task within an *agreed timespan*.

Clearly, after reorganization, the situation is similar to that of the first two examples, and the same course of action is now the rule: quality indicator(s) should be used to monitor progress.

It isn't nearly as easy as the above explanation might make out. It never is easy to bring about change in any organization, even using the established mechanisms, and here I am suggesting that they are not employed. For TQM to work efficiently, the forces for improvement must come primarily from those who benefit directly from the change.

For this to be possible, management must allow it to happen, the workforce must be trained to possess the skills to enable it to happen, and information must be freely and openly available to the workforce so that it can be seen to happen.

These conditions will not occur naturally; quite the contrary in fact. *Delegation, training and financial openness* will only come about with top management's *obsessive* support. That, simply, defines the role of the chief executive if total quality management is to be successful.

Responsibility must be passed down, and the role of management is to train and prepare the staff so that they are able to assume responsibility sensibly, then to keep a watching brief and provide guidance and encouragement. Unsupervised abrogation to an unprepared workforce is totally unacceptable, especially if it springs from an unconvinced management using it as a device to frustrate true delegation. The secret, again within the power of only the chief executive, is to persuade management of the critical importance of putting responsibility where it belongs, at the level of implementation. It goes without saying that adequate training must be given to all concerned: management in delegation skills; and the staff in specific work, organizational, problem-solving and reporting skills.

A layer, or layers, of the management and supervisory structure being stripped out is a sure sign that the *fruits* of delegation are being enjoyed, that bureaucracy is being reduced and, as a consequence, communications are improving. Reducing the number of layers of management demonstrates that a total quality management process is well under way.

Although the importance of training was expressed earlier, it cannot be repeated too often. A well-structured training programme is an integral part of the total quality management process. Clearly, training is essential if everyone in a company is to assume more responsibility and be more effective in what they do and how they cooperate with their colleagues. Like TQM, it must be a continuing process, because the pursuit of better quality is itself a continuing process. Companies are setting their sights on quality levels previously thought unrealistic (in many industries zero-defects is a concept that has real meaning!) and these higher standards demand better and better trained and motivated staff.

A first-class information system is fundamental to successful total quality management. As pointed out earlier, measurement is important because it plots progress, both at personal and company levels, and meaningful measurement is an integral component of the information system. Operators want, need, to know how their own internal business is progressing if their interest in quality improvement is to be sustained. If quality, or rather, lack of quality, can be measured, then it can be costed. The scale of the cost of non-conformance always comes as a shock. The first reaction is inevitably disbelief, but as the information is checked and refined, acceptance and a determination to substantially reduce the waste become the order of the day. *Knowing and appreciating the costs caused by lack of quality focus the attention of both management and staff.*

Business decisions must be financially justified, and, for this to be so, good, reliable, information is a precondition. Without financially based quality measurements it is impossible to choose objectively between competing materials, suppliers, designs and processes; or to justify better plant and equipment, more training and personnel development, and the best working conditions, etc.; yet many companies have been attempting just that. No wonder industry is scrambling to master the quality philosophy that has enabled certain firms and countries to catapult themselves into positions of seemingly unassailable world leadership.

This is no place to set out ways to cost lack of quality. The reader interested in learning more about the subject will find the theory and methodology described in British Standard, BS 6143.

At the personal level, operators should be plotting the movement of appropriate *quality indicators*. (This applies to all operators, whether they are employed in offices, production units, or field services.) These graphs must present a quickly visible history of the levels of conformance achieved by the process. An indicator must be agreed jointly by an operator and internal customer, must be simple to measure and reconcile between them, and be recorded by the operator. Indicators are useful only insofar as they enable a trend to be displayed; they are not intended to provide absolute measurement. Thus, keyboard errors, average time to answer a telephone, incorrect stores issues, products returned to assembler, incomplete order shipments, could be typical quality indicators. It is convenient if the plots record when and how processes are changed, so that the effects of the changes can be determined easily.

Everyone must understand also that quality indicators are intended to track the *performance of processes, not operators*. Management must consistently demonstrate its honesty by using indicators for this purpose only, and not be tempted to employ them as controls on operator efficiencies. Gaining, and retaining, the total confidence of the workforce is essential; total quality management is dependent on the reporting of honest information, and a degree of cooperation unusual in UK companies governed by established management structures and systems. Because it is the small, but continuous, improvement of processes that produces corresponding continuous improvements in quality, encouragement must be given to implementing changes to systems, procedures, methods and techniques, etc., which improve quality, and the significance of improving trends must always be acknowledged to the operators concerned. The process is continuous in more ways than one, because each modification and refinement affects processes further along the chain and, this in turn, begets still more change.

Driving for improvement through change, and attention to the minutest detail, is so much an integral part of the total quality process that, for many, better quality is synonymous with quality circles – worker panels that meet regularly to discuss how their sections can be improved. One can think of quality circles as both a device for encouraging *everyone to participate equally* in the quality process, and as a mechanism which improves quality through interlinking, endless chains of innovation and refinement. Quality circles flourish where companies provide appropriate levels of encouragement and support; conventional suggestion schemes, although capable of producing good ideas, must be regarded with caution, because they can be seen as working against the quality credo that everybody must *always* be seeking to improve the performance of the process.

The external customer is the one that makes all this effort worthwhile, and this fact must never be forgotten. The ripples of conformance requirements spreading out from the external customer provide the energy to drive the complex circles of internal customer/supplier improvement changes. One must be aware that these external customer demands are often not concerned with outstanding product features, but with *qualities* some-times, but erroneously, thought of as peripheral: clear but comprehensive literature, complete delivery when prom-ised, adequate installation and operating instructions, knowledgeable and polite service over the telephone. Every department, every employee, has a critical part to play in the quality profile of a company.

Embarking on a total quality management process is not to be undertaken lightly. It is not a question of simply employing just another in the latest line of management techniques. It demands obsessiveness from its senior management and a change to be wrought in the business culture, and encompasses all who work for the company. However, like most processes requiring significant application and energy, total quality management is capable of producing far-reaching, beneficial results. At the human level, work becomes a far more pleasant experience, while in business terms better quality leads inexorably to higher profitability and growth.

Total quality management constantly directs everyone towards the real, the only, reason for the existence of a commercial company: satisfying the needs of its custom-ers. This criterion cannot be satisfied by concentrating on *only* one area of the business, even if it is as important as improving relationships at the company/client interface. Indeed there is an argument that *superfical* customer care should be the last element tackled, not the first; that giving it priority is akin to corporate advertising, which projects glowing promises that cannot be reflected in reality. Customer care is about satisfying all the needs of the customer, by all the employees, in all the departments of a company, and that is nothing more than a definition of what total quality management is about. Customer care without total quality is a misnomer, if not a fraud.

8 Communication
Alfred Tack

Bad communication can lead to strikes, uncooperative suppliers, futile arguments, stress, production problems, time-wasting – all adversely affecting a customer-care policy. Let us now consider some of the major causes of errors in communication.

Listening

Listen and appraise

Only by mentally checking the words used by others can we be sure that we are interpreting their remarks correctly. Here are some examples of what people say, and what they really mean:

- 'It's the principle of the thing that counts, not the money!', which means, *It's the cash I'm concerned about.*
- 'I don't want to interfere', which means *I'm going to interfere, whether you like it or not!*
- 'Do you mind if I'm blunt?', meaning *Now I'm going to be bloody rude!*
- 'I know you won't object to me telling you . . .', meaning *Now you're going to get a piece of my mind!*
- 'Everyone knows . . .', meaning *On my way to the office a taxi driver told me.*
- 'To be perfectly honest with you . . .', meaning *I've been lying in my teeth all along – now I'm going to tell you half the truth.*
- 'I should think it would be obvious to the meanest intelligence', means *Now I'm going to bamboozle you with my erudition.*

- 'I had no intention of leaving the company, but I happened to bump into . . .', means *I've been studying the situations vacant columns for weeks.*
- 'Are you feeling all right?', means *You look as though you're on the last lap to me.*

To enable your mind to analyse the spoken words for their true meaning, you must be able to *listen carefully*. Simple? No – very hard. Talking is easy – listening very difficult. Few people listen intently. While others are talking, the non-listener racks his brain, searching for the telling phrase that will destroy the other person's argument, or win his respect.

The art of listening properly is to concentrate, and relax. No one listens with complete concentration, with pulses racing, fingers drumming, or fists clenched. The same applies to the half-listener, who sits forward on the edge of the chair, shoulders hunched, waiting to disagree violently with everything that has been said. By half-listening, he may lose the argument, in spite of his passionate belief that he is right.

To be a good communicator you have to recognize these non-listening signals, so that, if necessary, you can emphasize a point, or ask for confirmation that you have been understood. When it is your turn to listen, you must listen quietly, with no sense of urgency to interrupt.

Your aim, during every business discussion, union-problem policy argument, is to *hear, and understand exactly*, what the person means. Although others may interrupt you, you, as a good listener, must never interrupt them. Let the speaker talk himself out. Only when you know that he has fully communicated every point will you be in a position to communicate effectively yourself.

Does the trade-union convener listen intently to the personnel director? Equally important, does the personnel director listen intently to the trade-union convener? How many strikes might have been caused because one side or the other has not been listening intently to the arguments put forward? How well do *you* listen?

Don't rate yourself. Ask a colleague, or your wife, to rate you as:

1 Excellent.
2 Good.
3 Fair.
4 Poor.
5 Terrible.

Eight rules for effective listening

1 Concentrate harder when the speaker is boring, lacks enthusiasm, or speaks in a monotone. Do not mentally 'switch off' because of the extra effort required.
2 Never allow your anger to affect your listening capacity. Relax – you want to win an argument, a decision, a policy change, not a fight.
3 Take notes, if necessary.
4 Do not form a judgement until you have heard the whole proposal.
5 Listen intently for misstatements and generalizations. This will be to your advantage when it is your turn to speak.
6 Do not 'switch off' because you have 'heard it all before'. Be determined to hear it all again.
7 Listen intently for the facts. Often facts become almost engulfed in a mass of verbiage.
8 Do not allow distractions to interfere with your listening. Noises, telephones, flickering lights – any such distractions – should be excluded if possible, so that you can settle down and listen quietly.

The value of the voice

A manager who lacks the ability to speak clearly – mumbles, talks too quickly, or is hesitant in his speech – cannot be a totally effective communicator.

The quiet mumbler

Listening to him, you begin to wonder whether you are, at last, in need of a deaf aid. He swallows half his words, rarely raises his voice, and speaks in a monotone. He cannot communicate effectively, because no one can concentrate for long enough on what he is saying.

Do you recognize him? Good! Now compare yourself with him.

Do others regularly have to ask you to repeat your words? If you dictate to your secretary, does she have difficulty in hearing you? Do other people sometimes ask you to speak up? The quiet mumbler can overcome his problems by following the advice given later in this chapter.

The grasshopper

This is an example of a *grasshopper* attempting to express a point of view:

> . . . I want to discuss with you – and to settle right away – the question of cutting down staff. It seems ridiculous, doesn't it, to have to consider this when you remember that when Julie came for an interview we almost had to beg her to join us. But then, her uncle used to be in Bob's department, so that helped. What was his name? Oh yes I remember, it was Dick Long. He was a first-class designer, wasn't he – but then, art ran in his family. I was on holiday once with his brother Charlie – he was a classical musician; didn't play my kind of music at all, and I found him rather boring . . .

I have met many people who wander from one subject to another, and eventually forget the original point they wanted to make. Do you do that? Think of the *grasshoppers* you know so well in your organization, then compare youself with them. The test is simple enough.

Do you bring extraneous matters in when discussing a subject? Do you, while chatting to somebody, invariably introduce names of people they cannot possibly know, and tell some story about them?

In private life when we bore others with our *grasshopper* minds, we may lose friends. In business we can lose orders, goodwill, and respect.

The fast talker

With the fast talker it is a continual race between his thoughts and the revelation of them to others – a race he cannot win. But he tries so hard that at times he becomes almost incomprehensible – a professional gabbler.

Possibly the fast talker suffers from some form of anxiety complex, taking the form of a drive to keep talking at high speed in case his allotted time should run out and he won't be able to finish. Whatever the reason, psychological or otherwise, the fast talker is certainly not a good communicator. Much of what he says goes unheard by others, and the powers of concentration of those listening to him soon lapse.

The cure is difficult. To ask him to slow down is like suggesting to a golfer with a quick swing that he should slow his swing. The result, inevitably, is a series of jerks. Enthusiasts all tend to talk a little too quickly, but when one is discussing a business project, or an idea is put forward for consideration, if you want others to understand and be motivated by you, *you must slow down the pace at which you talk.*

The slow talker

It is as difficult to concentrate on the jerky sentences of the slow talker as it is on the quick-fire words of the gabbler. Even the most relaxed person becomes nervy when the slow talker pauses, speaks a few words, pauses again, then, with great deliberation, attempts to make his point.

Just as the listener believes a most important pronouncement is to be made there come the 'ahs', the 'ums', the 'you sees', the 'now let us considers', the 'I want to be deliberate about this', etc.

The slow talker often imagines himself to be the strong, silent type. To a listener, he is just a bore.

Compare yourself with the slow talker. It is far harder for the gabbler to slow down than it is for the slow talker to speed up – but the effort must be made.

The ventriloquist

These days, the dummy is the star of the ventriloquist's act. No longer do we look to see if the master's mouth is moving; now, we concentrate on the dummy.

But what if there is no voice throwing, no dummy – only a variety of sounds issuing from sealed lips, which we have to strain to hear? Then it becomes mostly a game of guesswork. Too many people try to emulate the ventriloquist, speaking with mouth almost tightly shut.

To speak clearly, your teeth must part and your lips open. It only needs practice and patience; but here are some rules to help you to improve your voice, whether you are a mumbler, a fast talker, a slow talker, or a ventriloquist. Since words are the essential material for speaking, and the voice is the instrument for shaping that material:

(a) Seek to improve both – to improve communication.
(b) This does not mean standardization of speech. Keep your brogue or dialect. Aim at bright, positive impact.

Try the following:

1 To improve your voice the first requisite is good stance, which gives self-confidence. You cannot breathe deeply and smoothly if you are hunched up.
2 Use deep breathing controlled by the diaphragm to ensure maximum motive power behind your words.

3 Practise flexible tongue movements.
4 Use vowels effectively. These sounds give beauty to speech, and aid audibility. A free-moving tongue and a flexible pair of lips are essential to their formation.
5 Good delivery is essential.
   (a) Try for natural pitch – no strain, or artificiality.
   (b) Use emphasis to help delivery by selecting the important words in any group.
   (c) Inflexion is an important ingredient, giving tone and variety, rise and fall.
   (d) Try for quality of tone; expression is at the heart of attractive speech. Tonal quality makes the voice sound enthusiastic, helps to express anger, sympathy, and all the emotions.
   (e) Variation of pace and effective pauses also help delivery.
6 Here are four suggestions for increasing the effective use of voice and words:
   (a) Practise deeper, controlled breathing.
   (b) Practise reading aloud for 10 minutes, every day.
   (c) Practise the use and formation of words, including one new word every day.
   (d) Practise projection – speaking forward.
7 Speaking effectively also means using words to greater advantage.
   (a) Phrasing correctly helps fluency.
   (b) Building a vocabulary means increasing word power.
   (c) Correct pronunciation (right accentuation) helps the effectiveness of words.
   (d) Avoid clichés, slang, technicalities for non-technical people, and avoid being pompous.

Speaking in public

Most managers have to address small meetings and, on occasion, large gatherings. Their effectiveness does not depend solely on the subject matter of their speech.

   Outstanding qualifications in engineering, medicine, accountancy, the law, are no guarantee that a knowledge-able person will be a successful communicator. A brilliant thesis could be ruined by an inability to speak fluently in public, while someone less able who can communicate well will receive applause and acclaim.

   Speaking effectively in public is not difficult to master. We have proved this over and over again at our courses, where many a manager has arrived almost tongue-tied, only to leave after a few days with not only the ability, but also the will – almost an eagerness – to speak in public.

   Here are some guidelines:

1 The average person can manage a reasonable conversation with one other person. When, however, an audience takes the place of that person – when the conversation becomes a presentation – many otherwise competent businessmen lose confidence in themselves. Why?
2 Nervous tension is one of the main barriers to effective speaking, and that tension is born of three fears:
   (a) Fear of failure.
   (b) Fear of looking foolish.
   (c) Fear of forgetting.
3 The practical way of dealing with these fears is by good presentation. If one knows how to prepare and present a talk, and finds a way of remembering what has been prepared, the battle is already half won. Remember the saying: *To fail to prepare is to prepare to fail.*
4 However, the manner and mannerisms of a nervous speaker result in visual distraction. When a speaker arrives, the audience will, in this order look, notice, and listen. When first appearing, therefore, always remember:
   (a) Smile, and look pleased to meet the audience.
   (b) Never appear hurried or flustered – take your time.
   (c) Survey the audience for a moment before you start.

5 Avoid mannerisms such as
   (a) Jingling keys or money.
   (b) Scratching your face.
   (c) Gesticulating for no purpose.
   (d) Swaying on your feet.
   (e) Fidgeting.
6 Never speak without notes, even if you do believe
   yourself to be word perfect.

Effective letter-writing

Is it worthwhile taking the trouble to ensure that every
letter posted, whether it be one seeking business,
answering a complaint, or requesting payment of an
account, is of high quality in layout, typing and content?

A nonsensical question! Most managers would agree
that letters should be, if not of the highest quality,
certainly of good standard. The facts are, however, that
about 30 per cent of letters we receive are dreadful, 30 per
cent below standard, 20 per cent standard, and 20 per cent
excellent.

Letters are *dreadful* because of misspelling, bad typing,
and ineffectiveness. *Below standard* letters are usually
poorly set out and include grammatical errors. They are
all of *I* appeal, instead of *you* appeal – *I* believe, *I* think, *I*
want, *we* produce, instead of *you* will be interested to
learn, *you* will be able to . . . They are also cliché-ridden.
The *average* letter is well written but still cliché-ridden,
and lacks warmth. The writer is apt to use six words
where two will do. The *excellent* letter follows the rules
given below.

The excuses for bad letter-writing are:

1 'Can't get good typists', which sometimes means 'Can't
   be bothered to check up and correct'.
2 'Haven't the time' (see Chapter 14, 'Time management').

3 'I'm no good at letter writing', which can mean 'I can't be bothered to learn'.
4 'I'm dependent on subordinates', which means no training scheme to improve the standards of letter-writing.

It is strange that when a manager is visiting a client, he will make sure that his appearance is immaculate; yet he will allow another of his company's ambassadors – a letter – to have such little appeal.

Bad communication by letters loses customers. Many service departmental managers write horrible, dictatorial letters, causing ill-feeling, producing a bad company image, and often failing in their objective.

You will, surely, have received at least one letter from a public utility corporation, a car manufacturer, a store, a local authority, which has infuriated you; so do *not* do unto others as they do unto you. Ensure that *every* letter sent out by you, your department, your company, is well received and enhances your company's reputation.

The mastering of effective letter-writing begins with the recognition and observance of three basic principles:

1 The need to define the *purpose* of the letter.
2 The need always to consider the *reader* of the letter.
3 The need always to use language *appropriate* to these two requirements. Fowler, in *Modern English Usage,* wrote, 'Anyone who wishes to become a good writer should endeavour, before he allows himself to be tempted by more showy qualities, to be DIRECT, SIMPLE, VIGOROUS, and LUCID'.

The following points are important:

1 *Be clear.* This means avoiding the ambiguous, making the correct use of punctuation, and placing adjectives and adverbs in the right context.
2 *Be concise.* Brevity is accomplished by the elimination of 'padding', caused most often through needless clichés and meaningless phrases.

3 *Be correct,* not only in facts, figures, data, detail, information, etc., but also in letter construction, i.e. grammar, punctuation, and especially spelling.

4 *Be complete.* This means providing all information and answers to satisfy the reader and the purpose of the letter.

5 *Be courteous.* Choice and use of words create the tone of the letter. The right tone will convey an image to the reader of a warm, helpful, interested human being. Make sure that the recipient's name is spelled correctly.

6 The layout of the letter must be neat and attractive.

7 Solid chunks of typing must be avoided. A simple rule of *one thought, idea, or subject, per paragraph* is a sound guide to follow.

8 Sentences should be kept as short as possible – not more than eighteen to twenty-five words makes reading and understanding easy.

9 Information of particular importance to the reader can be given emphasis by creating separate paragraphs, indented three or four spaces from the left-hand margin. These may be referenced alphabetically or numerically, or simply given additional attraction by an asterisk or a dash.

10 Production must be to the highest standard of typing. This standard will be set and maintained by the letter-writer. He must not accept alterations, overtyping, soiled stationery, erasure marks, or any other untidiness in typing.

11 More familiar and direct words should be used instead of commercial jargon; hackneyed phrases should be eliminated, and replaced by warmer, more expressive language.

12 The signature to a letter must always be personal, instead of *per pro,* or even worse, *p.p.*

13 Avoid using the footnote 'dictated by . . . and signed in his absence'.

14 Make sure that all enclosures *are* enclosed.

15 Identification of the writer should be clarified by having the name typed below the signature space and, where necessary or appropriate, his title and department.

16 Before replying to a letter, make sure that you have clearly understood the points raised or the questions asked.

If in doubt while dictating, always 'play back', or ask for a 'read back', and do not hesitate to make corrections at that time.

The essential in all communications is *to be understood* – and *to show understanding*.

Report-writing

The ability to write readable, informative, factual, concise reports is a most difficult, yet essential, form of communication. But are the majority of reports essential to the welfare of a business? The answer is *no*. All too often a report is requested:

1 As a delaying tactic.
2 To give somebody a job to do.
3 To show authority.
4 To make someone else feel important.
5 Because it is standard practice.
6 Because a committee doesn't know what action to take.

If therefore you are the authorizing person, always be quite objective, and consider these factors. Then ask yourself these questions:

(a) Is this report essential?
(b) Shall I read it carefully?
(c) Shall I take appropriate action?
(d) Will it be filed away to be read at some future date?

If you decide that the report is essential, give the 'go-ahead'. If not, think again. A brief discussion will often supply all the evidence required, without the time-wasting activities of unnecessary report-writing. Managers should be as ruthless in cutting down requests for reports as they should be in cancelling meetings.

Guidelines for report-writing

Why is the report required?

Is it to inform, to persuade, to help in decision-making, or for the purpose of reference at some later date? The report-writer must have these objectives clearly in mind before investigating, and then reporting; otherwise his report may be brilliantly written but only provide irrelevant information.

The request to be put to the authorizing person is, *'Please tell me exactly what you want from this report'*. Sometimes the authorizing person has not thought clearly about the objective of the report, and if this is not clear to him, the writer of the report cannot succeed in producing anything worthwhile.

Who is going to read the report?

If the readership is to be divided between technical and non-technical people, the writer will have to simplify many technical aspects of the report. If the reader is well versed in the technicalities, there will be no need to waste time emphasizing what is fully understood.

Research

To gather all the relevant information, the following questions should be answered:

(a) Which books, reports, research works, do I need to read?
(b) Whose advice should I seek?

(c) Whom must I interview?
(d) What areas must be visited?

Having found the answers to these questions, the report-writer must set time objectives, and adhere to them. Without such objectives report researching can continue for so long that the report is no longer useful by the time it has been completed. This happens regularly with reports requested by government ministers.

In the first place, merely list facts without making any assumptions or prejudging the issue. For example, when reading books, jot down only the relevant factors for later evaluation.

When interviewing someone who may be advising on, say, land mining, local traditions, ask only those questions pertaining to the objective of the report. Ignore generalities; only *facts* matter. Unsubstantiated claims have no place in a report.

Analysing information

Eventually the report-writer will have accumulated dozens, even hundreds, of facts. These now have to be classified; duplications are then deleted, and the remainder evaluated. This is quite a simple matter when a report-writer works systematically.

The analysis having been completed, the report-writer will then break down the main objectives into subsidiary objectives. For example, if a report is required on the advisability of opening a branch laundry in Exmouth, the subsidiary objectives might be to discover:

(a) Laundries now operating.
(b) The number of dry-cleaners in the vicinity.
(c) Local charges by laundries and dry-cleaners.
(d) Availability of staff.
(e) Availability of premises.
(f) Cost of building.

What the report-writer now has is a series of facts covering all the subsidiary objectives, to enable a final conclusion to be reached.

Writing the report

If the previous guidelines are adhered to, writing the report is relatively simple. The problem most report-writers face is a blank page and a blank mind. Ideas that abound while driving, original thoughts that percolate the dream world at night, and devastating comments that impinge on the mind while viewing TV, all seem to disappear when the time for writing arrives.

In speech-making, as you know, you only have to list a few facts and then elaborate on them. It is hard to originate, it is easy to amplify. If you are writing a report, you have only to elaborate on facts, just as you would if you were making a speech. Quite simple, really!

Language and style

Always write the report in the first person. It makes it so much more readable than when written in the third person. The rules of letter-writing apply equally to report-writing, but again, to cover them briefly:

1 Avoid clichés, jargon, unnecessary technicalities. Too many report writers attempt to build their own ego and, indirectly, their own qualifications, by using technical terms the reader has to check regularly.
2 Use short sentences.
3 Avoid emotional language.
4 Use plain and simple words, if possible – and remember, there is no poetic licence in report-writing.
5 Be positive, but not arrogant; and be sure that each paragraph deals with only one point.
6 Remember to be logical at all times.

Layout and supporting evidence

The whole layout of the report gives credibility to the author. Write only on one side of the paper, and leave a reasonable margin on the right-hand side to enable the reader to make notes where necessary. Double spacing will make the report easier to read.

Remember, few people enjoy reading reports, and if it is an ill-prepared and badly laid out report, the chances are that it will only be glanced at, while the well laid out, clearly written report can, undoubtedly, influence minds. That is what report-writing is about.

All supporting evidence that does not necessarily have to be included in the substance of the report should be given at the end. This may include graphs, charts, drawings, illustrations, and extracts from references quoted.

The summary

The report-writer should, finally, summarize his findings and state his conclusions and recommendations.

Noticeboards

That morning Arthur Jones had quarrelled with his wife, his youngest son had refused to go to school, and he had received a letter advising him of a surcharge payment to be made on a packaged holiday that he had booked. Arriving at work, he clocked in, and paused by the noticeboard to read the printed words on a sheet of yellow paper:

It has come to our notice that the NO SMOKING rule is being broken by employees using the toilets on the ground floor. In some cases, apparently, visits are solely for the purpose of smoking. This practice must cease forthwith. Anyone breaking the rule will be severely reprimanded and the misdemeanour registered. It must be realized that smoking on this floor incurs danger due to . . .

Does Arthur Jones immediately agree that the managers are right; or does he give vent to all his bottled-up anger over everything that has happened before he arrived at work?

'Why the hell shouldn't we smoke in there?' he asks a fellow worker. 'We're working for bloody dictators! They smoke wherever they like . . .' All his mates agree.

The workers know that the NO SMOKING rule is a safety factor, but everyone has been smoking in the lavatories for years, and with Arthur Jones, once emotion has taken over, it is not difficult for him to convince his mates that management merely wants to stop them having a quiet smoke in the comparative safety of the toilets.

If that notice is ignored, who is to blame – the workforce or management, which has been responsible for issuing the threat? The notice could have been written in a much more humane style. It would have said the same, but there would have been no ruffled feelings.

Before any notice is pinned on to a board, the writer should consider the feelings and views of those who will be reading it. Usually noticeboards are not good vehicles for listing misdemeanours. Provocative words such as the following should never be used:

(a) We can no longer tolerate . . .
(b) We must insist that . . .
(c) I have asked all managers to report to me if . . .
(d) Absenteeism is now averaging 10 per cent, and is having an adverse effect on productivity and profitability. Mrs Jones of Personnel has been asked to investigate all cases and report to management . . .

Such notices do not influence the minds of workers in favour of a management plea. We know that many newspaper editors and politicians keep urging management to take a tough stand (whatever that may mean) but toughness does not mean being dictatorially belligerent.

For example, in the notice referring to absenteeism, why waste the time of the majority of workers in reading a notice that applies only to a minority? The minority should be dealt with individually. There is no need for a notice to remind staff that absenteeism is high; it is action that is needed – not notices!

Clarity of notices

Whenever directives are issued or information given, management should ensure that no words or sentences can possibly have a double meaning. If a statement can be misinterpreted, it surely will be! That is how industrial problems are caused.

A careful check should be made for spelling mistakes or mistyped words. Any such mistakes will result in readers forgetting the message in their eagerness to belittle management. Keep each notice to one page – second pages are rarely read. Do not use coloured paper. Black on white makes for easier reading.

Do not continually use capital letters for emphasis. They serve no purpose, and often antagonize readers.

Never write a highly emotional notice while infuriated about something that you consider unfair. It could only cause anger subsequently without providing a solution, changing anything, or leading to a better relationship or understanding.

Siting of noticeboards

One central board, possibly adjacent to the staff entrance in a busy passageway, or adjacent to the staff canteen or entrance lobby, will result in many passers-by passing by without reading the notices. If anyone is late arriving or leaving the premises, if it is lunch time and everyone is hurrying to queue for food, notices will not be read carefully. Ideally there should be a noticeboard on every floor of an office block or factory, or in every department – and the notices should be duplicated. Main noticeboards should be reserved for social communications.

Attract attention

Too many notices are left on the noticeboards for too long, which results in passers-by glancing at, but not studying, them, on the assumption that there is nothing new to read. Notices should be taken down as soon as possible after management believes that the messages have been read by the majority of employees.

I have seen notices 2 or 3 months out of date still on boards. This happens when nobody is made responsible for taking down old notices. Someone should be delegated to inspect the noticeboards every day. It should not be necessary for any notice to remain on a board for longer than 7 days, unless of course there is a statutory obligation for the notice to be displayed at all times.

An effective idea is to use a red arrow that will adhere to the noticeboard, printed with the words *This is new*. Very few people will pass by without reading such an appeal. Although the noticeboards can never take the place of personal messages, they can, properly used, be good instruments of communication.

Briefing others

Every manager has, on occasion, to brief others to carry out delegated tasks. For example, when special duties have to be undertaken during holiday periods, often someone is asked to undertake a task for which he, or she, has little liking or understanding.

Delegates attending a negotiating session obviously have to be briefed. There are also briefing sessions before conferences and exhibitions, and an accountant may have to be carefully briefed before visiting a bank manager to discuss additional finance.

Briefing others is an important part of a management job, yet often it is treated almost casually. For example, when telling Bill what to do while Tom is on holiday, it is not enough to say, 'Oh you know what he does, Bill – just make sure the buying signals are checked regularly.'

But what happens if Bill is not certain of the action he should taken when the buying signals are set at *buy*? If Bill doesn't know exactly what to do, mistakes can occur.

If an accountant is told, 'Get the best possible rate; don't go too high,' what is *too high*? He may feel that he has pulled off a fine deal, but when the managing director returns, he may angrily denounce Bill for borrowing at such a high rate. To communicate effectively when briefing, these rules must be remembered:

1 Write down every factor relative to the briefing.
2 Explain the briefing factors slowly, and insist that subordinates do not rely on memory, but take notes.
3 Continually question subordinates, to make sure that they fully understand the notes they have taken.
4 Never accept, 'Don't worry – I know what to do!' Always reply, 'I shan't worry if you tell me exactly what you are going to do.'

Remember to carry out these rules whenever delegating, regardless of the fact that a subordinate may not take kindly to receiving instructions.

Communication boxes

Many organizations install suggestion boxes to enable employees to use their initiative and earn rewards for good ideas put forward; but the word *suggestion* is wrong. Suggestions are only a part of the communication process. What enlightened managers want to know is if their employees are satisfied with management. As well as their ideas for reducing costs, they also want to learn about their complaints. It is the 'niggles' that, if not discussed openly, give endless opportunities to the militants to cause trouble.

In a recent case a managing director received a letter from a disgruntled employee complaining bitterly of unfair treatment, and mentioning the fact that in her department there was a constant staff turnover, surely proving that something must be wrong. Some managing directors would not have accepted this criticism, and the bitterness in the department would have continued, but this particular managing director was not satisfied and made a deeper investigation.

The facts that emerged proved that Mrs X was right. The department manager was incompetent, and he knew very little about human relations.

There are, however, few employees who will write to their managing director, and perhaps even fewer managing directors who will take the trouble to investigate in depth. That is why the suggestion box should be renamed. It could be called

1 Your comment box.
2 Tell us box.
3 Speak up box.
4 We want to know box . . .

Such boxes will bring in the type of comments and suggestion that will really help industrial relations.

Communication is always two-way, and all too often management only communicates downwards. The *tell us* box is one way of achieving two-way communication.

The communicator

Public relations is an essential form of communication used by most successful organizations to teach, inform, and guide. While a PRO can enhance the image of a good company, he cannot build the image of a company of less repute; he cannot solve problems of industrial relations, but he can help to build company loyalties. And, most certainly, a good PRO can get publicity for a company's caring attitude towards its customers.

Good communications between supplier and buyer, between management and employee, and for all negotiators are essential ingredients in the ultimate objectives – customer care.

Gobbledegook

At the moment there is some competition between two quality newspapers as to who can publish examples of unbelievably bad letters, almost incomprehensible information sheets, and difficult-to-follow instruction manuals. There is an insistence that there is really no need to use so much jargon. Letter-writing has been covered in previous chapters, but service departments are sometimes the worst offenders when issuing instructions and service manuals that only the service manager himself understands.

This is an example of anti-customer care. A customer sweating to erect a kitchen cabinet unit and failing to do so because the instructions are so difficult to follow doesn't believe that these instructions could be written by an employee of a caring company.

It is rare to find such a manual written in simple, plain English that can be easily understood.

I urge those who compile such manuals and instructions leaflets to have them checked by someone who is not an employee of the company before they are used on frustrated customers. They will learn the truth, which they would never learn from associates who are daily users of the jargon. What is so clear to the solicitor or accountant is sheer muddle to a client without training in such professions. Demand clarity in all directions for use, instruction manuals and all printed matter sent to customers.

9 Difficult customers
James Hiney DMS

*Director and General Manager, TACK Training
International Ltd*

Whatever the old adage may have you believe, everyone knows that the customer is *not* always right. But it is a good point to start from, because your aim is to ensure that every one of your customers who has any kind of problem feels better after the encounter than before. This may be simple enough even for the least experienced customer-handler when faced with a friendly client or customer who is prepared to be reasonable, but how to cope when faced with someone who can loosely be described as a *difficult customer* is a different question.

How would you define a difficult customer? 'Someone who is always making a fuss about nothing'. Really? About nothing? Now wait a minute, he's not the most difficult; at least he is giving you a chance to put things right. The really difficult customer is he who never says he is dissatisfied but simply closes his account. The Ford Motor Company sends a questionnaire to everyone who buys a car from them asking about aspects that a customer might not be happy with, might not complain about, but might remember when next buying a car. Perhaps only a tiny point could tip the scales of decision. Ford follow up replies by telephone – 'Thank you for completing our questionnaire; glad everything went so smoothly' or 'Sorry to hear you had a problem; let's arrange to put it right . . . by the way, I'd hate to think we'd ignored a complaint; did you mention it to anyone here before filling in our questionnaire?' '*No, I didn't like to make a fuss.*'

However vociferous they may be to their friends, relatively few people enjoy complaining to the company concerned, which then at least would have the chance of dealing with the problem. Two factors determine whether or not a complaint will be made – the physical and the mental attitude. Physically is it a simple task to take the offending article back, in terms of distance, cost and time? Should I write a letter (I am not very good at writing letters); would it be better to telephone (will they palm me off with excuses)?

The same applies to business-to-business transactions. Company A is not really satisfied with the goods or services supplied by Company B, so they buy from Company C next time. Why should this happen? The offers made by B and C were hardly distinguishable, *'but I wasn't really happy with B last time'*, thinks the buyer. He didn't complain because it would have been making a fuss about not very much. He didn't talk about it to his colleagues – he may even have brushed aside their comments or enquiries – because he didn't want them to think he didn't have his finger on the pulse. He didn't mention it to his boss, as he feared he might have to explain why the specification of the goods or services supplied hadn't been drawn up more precisely.

Even where there is justifiable cause for complaint, most people dislike complaining. They have to 'psych' themselves up to complain, and then very often swing to the other extreme – from not wanting to say anything to wild exaggeration. When the recipient of the complaint lets it be seen that it is obviously exaggerated, the pendulum may continue its swing (to even greater aggression) or reverse itself (to talking themselves out of the complaint). They then feel aggrieved – at themselves, for poorly expressing the points they wanted to make, and at the other party (you or me), for not understanding, not listening properly, not taking any action, not taking the *right* action anyway. After that it's only a very small step to 'I've never been really happy with that company' and an even smaller one to 'I shall not deal with them again'. And you thought difficult customers were always making a fuss?! The rest of this book is devoted to making sure that the 'silent majority' become regular customers, lifelong friends of your company. The rest of this chapter is devoted to those fuss-makers, of one sort or another.

So where shall we start? How about beginning with the aggressive person – 'He-who-thoroughly-enjoys-complaining-at-every-opportunity'? You've met him, I know. If there really isn't any justification, he will manufacture one: 'Your receptionist was rude' (being new she did not recognize him and had the effrontery to ask him to sign the visitors' book); 'Your gatekeeper wouldn't let me park' (he arrived during a fire practice when the entire staff was in the car park and didn't listen to the explanation). If you know he *always* finds something to complain about, should you treat him in any way differently from the genuine complainer? If so, *how* differently? Should he have more attention? ('It's so-and-so again – give him whatever he wants to keep him quiet, he's always complaining.') Or does he deserve less attention? ('What a nuisance he is – whatever we do for him it isn't enough.')

So, more or less attention than other people? Well *more* is what those who throw their toys out of the cot often get, and as long as other customers are not being neglected – *priority* should be reserved for a matter of great importance – does it matter? Our task is to *satisfy* him if humanly possible, as it is when anyone complains. It's just that we hear from him so often that it's easy to think 'Not him again!' Don't allow yourself (or indeed, him) to trivialize his complaints simply by their frequency. Something is not right, whether we hear about one complaint from each of five customers or five complaints from just the one, and when we trot out the old cliché 'Thank you for bringing this problem to our attention,' we should mean every syllable.

However trivial a complaint appears at first sight, there may be a kernel of truth in it. Perhaps no offence was intended, but a poor choice of words can transform the perceived meaning. There is an enormous difference, for example, in telling a lady that her new hat is out of this world and saying it looks like nothing on earth. However unintentionally, was that receptionist rude? That gatekeeper awkward? However jaundiced we may feel, complaints should be welcomed as they highlight *a problem* – a problem of quality or of customer care. It is our responsibility to put things right, which doesn't necessarily mean doing whatever outlandish thing the complainer demands! But it does mean reacting to the complaint in a disciplined, *professional* manner, however he chooses to present it.

Act quickly

If he writes, speed is essential; a telephone call *today* is even better than a reply by return of post, which is the least he can expect. If he arrives on your premises, take him somewhere private quickly. There is nothing quite like an audience for magnifying a problem (nor, of course, for being put off from buying themselves). If he telephones, give him your undivided attention, however busy you may be; time taken now may go some way, perhaps a long way, towards defusing the situation. Listen carefully, make notes, but *don't interrupt* – interruptions only fan the flames. Allow him to let off steam, and when he eventually begins to flag, tell him you are sorry to hear about his complaint (which is true!) before asking the questions that are usually necessary, to give you a rounded picture of the problem. In most cases you will have to investigate further, and provided you can get back to the complainer reasonably quickly, the empathy you have been showing will have won you a long enough breathing space.

Get the facts

When you have got the facts, you have to decide what objectives the complainer had. He may have told you, perhaps in no uncertain terms, but very often people just want to get things off their chests. So what must you do to turn him (back) into a satisfied customer. There is no snappy answer – no panacea for all seasons, as it were – but there is a simple routine you can follow. During the first contact, when you listened to (or told him that you had read – and possibly had to listen to him repeat what he'd written about) his complaint, he may well have been quite emotional, so you didn't use logic, only empathy. You know the truth of the saying: 'No one ever won an argument with a customer'. But after your investigation you can afford to present a logical case, which naturally will depend on the facts, and on company policy. For example, many companies limit their liability in case of goods proving to be defective to replacement of the sub-standard item(s), so *you do not have the authority* to offer to pay for the costs (allegedly) incurred for damage to his equipment or materials. But if you could send a replacement by express courier, for example, this would be a small cost compared with losing a customer.

Always be fair

Of course you have to be careful to sort the sheep from the goats – those with a genuine complaint from the try-it-on brigade. Your investigation should help, but there are always those grey areas when you can never be quite sure of the facts. Within the limits of your company policy, if in doubt err on the generous side – remember you are seeking a *satisfied* customer. But be careful; it's always easier to give something away ('We'll cancel the charge') than to appear tough. Don't make the mistake of becoming 'soft' simply because it is easier than saying, in effect, 'You don't have a justifiable complaint.' Polite but firm should be your watchword in these circumstances. But also be careful not to miss the genuine complainer who expresses himself badly and so seems to be trying it on. Brushed aside, however politely, he may feel even more aggrieved – he has a complaint and no one will put it right, and another (potentially) regular customer is steered towards the competition.

Ask the right questions

Help your complainer by asking 'closed' questions, which demand a yes/no answer, or 'limited choice' questions – 'Was it this or that?' – rather than the more useful, information-eliciting 'open-ended' questions, which start with what? when? how? who? They can come later when he has relaxed a little, and before you start probing with 'why?'

Of course someone can be an ill-at-ease difficult customer without having a genuine complaint. Could it be that he didn't understand what his boss wanted him to ask us? A breakdown of communication between them that his boss failed to notice? (If this occurs, it's always the senior person's ultimate responsibility, though of course our contact should have plucked up enough courage to say that he hadn't understood.) Or perhaps they have had a quotation from one of our competitors and want us to give them the opportunity of being able to say they can 'get it cheaper elsewhere'. Or, if we turn out to be more expensive than the other fellow, to say to their senior management that they 'obtained several quotes' before buying. The treatment? As before, closed and limited choice questions first and open-ended questions only when you have relaxed him.

Clarify the position

Have you ever taken something for overhaul or repair – a car for service perhaps – and, not being technically too competent, have had difficulty in explaining what's wrong? 'It's a squeak,' you say. 'Well, perhaps not a squeak, more a squeal, and it comes from somewhere under the bonnet on the right hand side . . .' But when you get it back, the problem is still there ('They charge the earth for servicing your car, but they don't want to know about anything out of the ordinary; they only want to do what the book says they should do on each service – *assuming they do do what they are supposed to do* – I don't know enough to check up.')

Similarly ignorant is the person who 'can't quite describe' what he wants; indeed, 'doesn't even know if you make it, but he's seen something like it somewhere'. You may not be able to help him of course, but you'll never know if you brush him off too sharply. Show your natural interest in this unusual problem and your concern – anxiety even – to be of service. Open-ended questions to start – remember, when? what? how? who? – followed by the probing why?, and checking your understanding all the way with mini-summaries. At the end you may find you still can't help, but, handled well, he may feel that your company are good people to do business with, and an enquiry for something you couldn't do may lead to orders that you most certainly can fulfil. And if no one else says it, let me: well done!

If the ignorant person is a difficult customer, what about his opposite number, the knowledgeable customer. As bad as a complainer, in showing off to any audience, he'll take a lot of your time explaining why your product is made in precisely the way it is, or in demanding enlightenment from the world at large why it isn't made differently. Maybe he really is an expert, maybe not. But it is no part of our brief to show up any weak spots, nor to prove (to our own satisfaction, if not to his) that we know *even* more about it than he.

Perhaps you suspect you didn't know enough on this occasion. Don't try to 'flannel'. If you don't have to say it too often, it's not weakness to admit that someone is taking you out of your depth. Of course choice of words is again important. Saying, for example, 'Mr X, I can't pretend to in depth technical knowledge of this unit. Could I arrange for one of our design engineers to speak to you about it?' would show a caring attitude. He may be difficult enough to decline this offer, in which case you should *listen* even more *carefully*, if that is possible, and make notes of what you are told, as well as of those casual throw-away comments which help you to get the whole picture in any conversation. Give him the extra opportunity of showing off (to you) by checking frequently on your understanding. Above all, if he is placing an order, check the catalogue numbers and descriptions as well as prices while you are still in contact.

You may have noticed, especially if you sometimes also buy for someone else, that many shops now train their staff to tell you what you are buying before entering the details into the computerized till. 'That's one shirt size 16 and one 15½, both at £Z' they say (and imply, 'You did realize they were different sizes didn't you?'), clearly giving you the opportunity of avoiding another journey to exchange the wrong one if you've made a mistake. Make absolutely certain that you do the same – *especially* with the knowledgeable customer.

The 'been-around-a-long-time, seen-it all, know-what-I-want' character *may* be a difficult customer, but it is often a hard shell concealing a marshmallow centre. Yes, he's experienced; *use* his experience. If it's true, let him see that you too have some experience in the business (but *never* as much as he has, naturally!). Open-ended questions about the changes he has seen over the years will usually get him talking, and careful listening will enable you to use *your* experience to zoom in on any point he makes, or even throws away, which could be useful in achieving your objective. Once you have got him started, he may become akin to another difficult customer – the non-stop-talker – but happily the best way of handling *him* is only likely to add to the experienced customer's growing esteem of you as a sensible person who actually listens to (and tries to learn from) someone with more experience! And because you are patently so willing to learn, isn't he likely to see you as a good person to do business with because 'I can talk to that person'?

The way to cope with the talkative customer – 'non-stop' isn't really accurate, as even the most inveterate chin-wagger has to pause occasionally, if only for breath – is to hit him (in boxing parlance) with 'the old one-two'. Recognizing that attempting to interrupt him would be futile, as well as plain bad manners, wait until he pauses for breath – and even then you'll have to be quick – and hit him with One, his name, and Two, 'You said something a moment ago that I found particularly interesting . . .' The use of his name checks him just long enough for you to show interest, and very few people could resist finding out what was so interesting, could they? By his very nature, he will be off again as soon as he has established what interested you, so sit back and wait for an opportunity of repeating the 'one-two' process: name and interest, and again, and again! But gradually he too will warm to you simply because everyone around him is so used to the wall of words with which he surrounds himself that long ago they gave up listening and so never hear anything interesting in what he says. But you *listen* and find what he says of *interest*, using what he has said as a foundation for leading the conversation gently to your objective.

If the talker is difficult, what about his exact opposite, the taciturn, largely uncommunicative, Trappist monk of a customer? Obviously not totally silent, he has been known to break into a monosyllabic grunt on occasions, but very few people have ever been able to hold a conversation with him. This may be because he dislikes conversation or because he is shy, and therein lies your difficulty. If he doesn't *like* talking, he won't thank you for making him do so. If he is *shy*, he may be pleased to have met someone he *can* talk to. Which is he? Can you tell? Does it matter, because he is very unlikely to become a properly cared for customer if you and he never speak. So go for broke with open-ended questions kept strictly to business topics. Use 'signposting' techniques – 'So that I can establish which level of service you are likely to require, I'll need to ask some questions about the geographical locations of your UK and overseas clients. For example, . . .' Don't venture away from the formal unless and until he gives a strong lead in that direction. Of course he doesn't *have* to reply, but it's difficult not to do so. Don't be surprised if he has reverted to type when next you speak to him. He is never likely to become a brilliant conversationalist, but may well talk to you more than to most; and just think, if shyness is his problem, you may have helped him to a fuller life – truly, customer care.

The essence of caring for some customers is to realize that they prefer to look at *things* rather than *people*; to be shown around the factory or the site. Show them whatever you have to show, to prevent their becoming difficult later.

Even more than with the previous difficult customer, however, your unobtrusive – firm and friendly – marshalling of the conversation and of him will be needed for the poor chap who has the authority but not the ability to make up his mind. As soon as you have identified him – you probably used a simple alternative and it was patently too much for him – you have to put ideas into his mind with leading questions: 'Would I be right in thinking . . .', 'I imagine your budget for this project isn't inexhaustible, so wouldn't it be best if we looked at it this way . . .?' At the end of the conversation he'll be convinced that he decided each point (which in fact he did) and that he came to the most logical conclusion. What could be better customer care than that?

Summary

To summarize this chapter and to provide you with an action plan for satisfying a difficult customer, remember to:

1 Listen carefully to what he or she is saying, including those seemingly inconsequential, throw-away remarks.
2 Note down the main points ('You won't mind my making notes to ensure that I have a clear understanding' would be a small additional courtesy).
3 Ask questions:
   (a) Open-ended questions – who? what? when? how?
   (b) Limited choice questions – which?
   (c) Probing questions – why?
   (d) Leading questions – 'Would I be right in thinking . . .?'
   (e) Closed questions – asking for a yes/no response.
4 Get the facts from the above questions. Once you have them, you will be in a position to clarify the position.
5 Clarify the position, finally, from both points of view.

When dealing with a complaint, remember also that your speed of response is vital. To minimize any additional irritation, which would certainly be generated by delay on your part, *act quickly* – preferably by an immediate telephone call, followed, if necessary, by a letter. In negotiating a settlement, *always be fair.* Your prime concern should be to re-establish goodwill and to retain a (now once more) satisfied customer.

10 Customer care and service
Peter Brown
Associate Director, TACK Training International Ltd

The service engineer – special agent

Anyone who has ever worked with service engineers will know that they are special people. They are different from those engineers who do similar jobs in factories, and in industry in general. What is it that makes them different? How can anyone enjoy working under continual pressure; working with the customer looking over their shoulder; knowing that the job is always required 'half-an-hour ago'?

Quite simply, it is that they enjoy being 'in the front-line', facing the customer. They know that they have a special relationship with their customers; they are the Seventh Cavalry of industry, appearing over the horizon at the moment of greatest need; they are confidants, always prepared to lend a sympathetic ear. Above all, at every call they put into practice all the objectives of customer care.

The roles of the service engineer

What is the role of the service engineer? How does he or she maintain the difficult balance between the interests of the employer (whom they see occasionally) and the customer (whom they see regularly)? What qualities must this paragon possess?

There are five crucial roles which the service engineer should be capable of playing. Each must be instilled with competence and professionalism.

The technician

Technical competence, at any level of engineering, is gained through a mixture of training and related experience. The majority of service engineers are skilled in their particular trades, and experience has always been an essential part of the job description. It is rare to meet a service engineer who is not technically competent, but, like most good things in life, this does bring its attendant problems.

We have all met the engineer who knows the solution long before we have finished explaining the symptoms. There is also the over-confident fellow who believes that his knowledge and experience are so superior to ours that he brushes aside our opinions and, by doing so, puts us down – the very antithesis to customer care. It is essential that the service engineer develops a broader view *and* a sensitivity to the behaviour of others.

The company representative

Service engineers will usually have more direct contact with the customer than any other company employee. Everything about their appearance and their activities represents an image of their employer – the condition and cleanliness of their vehicle, their working clothes, their tool-kit, their working practices.

When under pressure, it is tempting for the engineer to use 'the boss', 'the stores', 'the salesman', as an escape route, without realizing the long-term damage that he is inflicting on the hand that feeds him. It also saps the confidence of the customer in the company.

The salesman

There are a number of clearly identifiable areas where selling is accepted as an essential part of customer service:

the provision of replacement parts, the setting up of maintenance contracts, all for the benefit of the customer. Surely the best way an engineer can guarantee his own continued employment is by maximizing the sales of his own company's products.

The researcher

Expensive research projects are designed to simulate actual work conditions, but regularly fail to match the real wear and tear imposed by real people with real production targets to meet. The service engineer is able to gain first-hand knowledge of product performance and problems, and discuss such matters with the actual end user.

He can then pass any significant matters back through the correct channels. Few people would argue with this simple logic, but many engineers remain blind to the information available to them, which can benefit both customer and company. They do not see themselves as a communications link between the customer and the manufacturer. It is not uncommon to find engineers who will cheerfully continue to repair faults that could be totally cured by a simple design modification.

Some will incorporate their own modifications without informing their own management. One particularly conscientious engineer, who was concerned about complaints of noisy equipment, decided that the problem could be solved by installing additional insulating material around the outer casing. It was only by chance that his own manager heard of this and, checking the material, found that it was liable to burst into flames at a temperature lower than that at which the equipment regularly operated. A major disaster could have resulted from the engineer seeing himself as a one-man band rather than a member of a team.

It is essential to report back on all corrections that are not standard.

The educator

In many industries it is a sad fact that operator training falls well short of a level necessary to maximize equipment performance. Even where there is mandatory training, e.g. the certification of drivers of fork-lift trucks, this is aimed more at achieving minimum safety standards rather than improving productivity. The service engineer's unique combination of opportunity and expertise could be used in an advisory capacity, to maintain long-term product improvement – to the ultimate benefit of the customer.

Attributes, skills and knowledge

It would be extremely optimistic and naive to expect that sufficient proficiency in the five major roles listed above exists in all aspiring and practising service engineers. We have agreed that they are a special sort of people, in that they possess technical competence, are loyal employees and are, certainly, customer-orientated. On the other hand, it is these very strengths that may well create weaknesses in key areas, such as company representation and customer-awareness.

In order to identify and develop the truly professional service engineer we still require a clearer understanding of precise selection and training criteria. These can be classified under three key headings:

A ATTRIBUTES
S SKILLS
K KNOWLEDGE

Attributes

An engineer patiently listens to a customer's tale of woe. He has heard it many times before, and knows much of it is not factual. This ability to be patient and sympathetic is an attribute related to personality and character, and will have developed partly as a result of natural style, and partly as a result of life's experiences. For this reason it is a quality that is best identified during the selection process. It is not surprising that many companies prefer to develop service engineers through their internal apprenticeship and training schemes, as this removes much of the guesswork.

Because of their long-term nature, attributes cannot easily be changed, but they can be modified or conditioned if there is sufficient willingness and guidance. Later in this chapter we list some of the main characteristics of behaviour, and show how increased understanding can help the development process.

Listed below are a number of the leading attributes that have been identified by engineers attending TACK training courses:

CONFIDENCE	HELPFULNESS	FRIENDLINESS
DIPLOMACY	SENSITIVITY	UNDERSTAND-ING
SYMPATHY	COURTESY	PATIENCE
GOOD HUMOUR	POSITIVENESS	ENTHUSIASM

Skills

Skills are both learnable and transferable. An engineer entering a technical training course and having the necessary aptitude will be able to acquire a range of logical skills that, once learned, will be useful in a wide range of circumstances. In most cases there is no specifically right or wrong way of using these skills. For instance, two engineers asked to repair a certain component might use completely different methods; and in both cases the result is a satisfactory job.

In the broader context of customer care, behavioural skills are as important as technical skills. It is the ability to handle difficult *people* situations that differentiates the service engineer from his factory-based counterpart. It is the manner in which they are handled that separates the good service engineer from the ordinary.

Knowledge

Knowledge is the most straightforward of qualities. It is logical, can be learned, and is either right or wrong. For instance, either my company offers a planned maintenance programme or it does not. It cannot be subject to individual discretion.

If the necessary levels of knowledge are to be achieved and maintained, then two major requirements must be fulfilled. Firstly, the engineer needs to be aware of the need for such knowledge; and, secondly, but possibly more importantly, company management must provide the right opportunities for its acquisition. The manner of fulfilling this second requirement can vary from providing easy access to information, e.g. updates on company policy, products, prices, etc., to the running of regular training sessions.

The areas of knowledge shown in Table 10.1 have been identified as those needed by a service engineeer in his day-to-day activities.

ASK – self-assessment

Table 10.1 lists only the more general qualities required by service engineers. It would be a simple matter to add

Table 10.1

Products/services	Company policy	Company systems
Availabilities	Products	Parts
Advertising	Competition	Geography
Legal requirements		

further, equally important, items. Some companies or industries might have qualities that are specific to them.

So far we have claimed that this approach offers two major benefits. It could certainly help in the drafting of selection criteria, and in the preparation of induction training programmes. An additional, and equally valuable, use would be self-assessment by those who are already service engineers.

At the end of this chapter there is an 'ASK' questionnaire, which can be used to assess present levels of attributes, skills, and knowledge as good, quite good, or poor. First, make sure that all the qualities necessary for your company and industry are included in the lists, then assess your own or your teams' current abilities by ticking the relevant column. Absolute honesty, not wishful thinking, is essential.

What can we do about behaviour?

It will be of little use assessing current ability levels unless it is possible to make improvements in those areas rated 'quite good' or 'poor'. Fortunately, skills and knowledge should present little or no difficulty. Much of this book is devoted to customer-related skills. Equally, most of the knowledge that is required should be freely available to any engineer who is prepared to make the effort.

The ASK questionnaire can be used by managers as a checklist to ensure that the necessary information and encouragement are provided.

That brings us to attributes that are related to personality and character.

What can be done to develop or improve here? It will certainly help if we forget many of the myths that surround our behaviour. We can start by examining the three basic principles of behaviour:

1 Behaviour is learned.
2 Behaviour is controllable.
3 Behaviour is reactive.

Behaviour is learned

From the moment we are born we learn to adopt the behaviour patterns that are most likely to give satisfactory results. The way in which an engineer behaves will have developed from thousands of such learning situations.

The one problem we face is that, as adults, we sometimes assume that we know it all. To accept and reintroduce the learning process will be difficult, but it is by no means impossible. The first step is to examine our actions in the context of customer care, and to decide which new behaviour patterns we wish to learn.

Behaviour is controllable

It is often convenient to blame others for the way in which we behave. In fact we have total control over our behaviour at all times, and have no one else but ourselves to blame if it is less than professional.

It is natural and normal for an engineer to choose a manner which 'mirrors' that of the customer. Friendly, cheerful customers will be greeted in a friendly, cheerful way. Those who are taciturn and dogmatic are likely to receive similar treatment in return. In both cases the engineer is subconsciously choosing his behaviour.

Anyone who deals with customers should carefully check their behaviour against their ASK questionnaire, and remember that they do have a choice in the way that they behave.

Behaviour is reactive

While the engineer is 'mirroring' the customers' behaviour, the customers themselves are reacting to the way in which they are being treated. Both reactions are completely subconscious, but the combined behaviours can easily dominate the original situation. The engineer who develops the ability to choose or control his behaviour enjoys the double advantage of also influencing the behaviour of the customer.

Behavioural styles

In every walk of life there are people who can ease or even solve difficult situations simply by their ability to develop good working relationships. Such people have usually taken the trouble to consider and modify their behaviour.

Consider the following situations:

Customer: 'Why are your products so unreliable?'
How should the engineer reply?

(a) 'They're not! They're as good as anything else in the market!'
(b) 'Sorry about the trouble you've had; believe me, it is most unusual, but I've given it a good check and I'm certain it will be OK now.'
(c) 'I wouldn't know about that. I only service them.'
(d) 'I'm really sorry you've been so unlucky with this one. I know it isn't the top of the range, but there are plenty worse. I don't know why it has given so much trouble.'

That one is easy. The second answer is more likely to be effective. But why is it effective? There are three good reasons for its likely success:

(a) The customer does not feel put down. He has a right to be annoyed, and the engineer accepts this.
(b) The engineer has expressed his own point of view and is loyal to his company and its products, but he chooses a passive reply, which has a calming effect. He does not mirror the customer's anger.
(c) The engineer offers an immediate and acceptable solution. If there is a solution that will suit both

parties (in most cases there is, for the engineer and the customer both want the machine to be working again as soon as possible), then the engineer should search for it. If neither party is aggrieved or has lost face, then we have a win/win. Two satisfied people.

Customer: 'Why are your charges so high?'
  How should the engineer reply?

(a) 'Prices are nothing to do with me, so I can't comment.'
(b) 'They're not high when you compare them with our competitors. None of them could give you this service at a lower price.'
(c) 'I know they are a bit on the high side, but they keep telling me that overheads are increasing all the time. I suppose someone has to pay.'
(d) 'They aren't bad when you compare them with the cost of downtime. We find that customers like yourself rely on a quick response, and recognize that such a service is good value for money.'

Which of these answers satisfies the three principles set out above? Clearly, in the first reply the engineer totally avoids the problem, which, in this case, helps no one. In the second the engineer's determination to defend his own company results in an implied attack on the customer's point of view, and invites argument. The third reply might work, but it verges on the 'soft-option'; it partly evades the issue, and lacks confidence. The last offers the best chance in that the engineer defends his employer's point of view, and uses a factual argument based on the customer's interests. Another win/win?

The A, B, C and D of behaviour

In both examples shown above the engineer achieved a compromise, maintaining a balance between loyalty to his own employer and the needs of the customer. As both parties are satisfied, such an outcome would be acceptable in most situations, but it would be wrong to rely on one particular style for all circumstances.

It is very convenient that, for the purposes of customer care, we can summarize a broad range of styles under four main headings – the A, B, C and D of behaviour.

A = Avoiding

As the description suggests, this style should be the least used of all, but there will be situations where avoiding a problem is best for both the engineer and the customer. Take the following example:

Customer: 'That new engineer has rather a quick temper, hasn't he?'
Engineer: 'I really can't say – I hardly know him.'

In this instance, to defend the other engineer or to agree with the customer could be equally dangerous. As can be seen, where discretion is required, avoidance is likely to be the safest style.

It must be stressed that the apparent ease with which difficult situations can be avoided should not encourage anyone to adopt this style as a popular escape route. It can be seen in the two examples in 'Behavioural styles' above that answers (c) and (a) respectively adopt an avoiding style. Both fail because they avoid an issue that is important to the customer. The roles of troubleshooter and company representative, as well as the needs of customer care, will mean that the majority of cases require more positive handling.

B = Bountiful

The dictionary defines bountiful as 'generous', 'liberal'. In business terms 'goodwill' might be more accurate, as this provides a clearer indication of where this particular behavioural style fits into the service scene. Occasionally it does make sense to do a favour or to offer something beyond the normally accepted levels of service:

Customer: 'If you haven't got it in your van-stock, how long will I have to wait?'

Engineer: 'Don't worry, I can pick it up from the depot this evening, and drop it off first thing in the morning.'

An excellent example of customer service, which suggests that the bountiful approach can play an important part in the service function.

Whenever it is possible to do the customer a special favour, the customer-care policy is seen in action. Better for an engineer to 'put himself out' than to have an aggrieved customer.

C = Compromising

The two examples in 'Behavioural styles' above provide good examples of compromising in action. As the name implies, compromising gives a balanced outcome that preserves the rights of both parties. It would certainly be wrong for the customers to feel offended, or that their problems were not receiving sympathetic treatment. On the other hand, the engineer must be prepared to stand by his company and its policies:

Customer: 'Why don't you ever have the right parts with you when you come to do repairs?'

Engineer: 'I understand your concern and I shall certainly mention it to the boss when I get back, but I've just checked, and this is only the second time in the last year that I have not had the right parts. But I do agree that it's two too many.'

It is even more important than usual that the engineer is telling the truth as a statement based on fact is hard to dispute. The compromising style is a bread-and-butter approach, suitable for many occasions. It will often be found in practice that even where other styles are used, they contain an element of win/win or compromise.

D = Determined

It is, perhaps, fitting that the determined approach comes last on the list, as for most customer situations it should be the last resort. Circumstances do arise where the customer asks for the impossible, and it is necessary to make a stand.

Customer (being insistent):	'I'm certainly not signing for three hours labour charge. You were only working on the machine for two hours. The rest of the time you were on the phone!'
Engineer:	'I am sorry, but the phone calls were necessary, to check out some technical details with the factory. I'm sure you will understand that the time was devoted to your repair, and agree that the hours will have to stand.'

Determined does not mean aggressive or take-it-or-leave-it. It is still necessary to remain courteous and demonstrate an awareness of the other's point of view. The engineer may be correct but being correct is not always enough. The customer has a right to query the charge and the handling of the repair. In these situations, the main behavioural skill lies in listening first then explaining – not imposing – the preferred solution.

Behaviour – the right of the matter

It has already been stated that professional use of behaviour means that we are always striving to strike a balance between conflicting needs – or *rights*.

On the one hand, there are the rights of the customer. On the other hand, there are the rights of the engineer and his employer. This idea of 'equal rights' may sound strange in an environment where it is usually deemed that 'the customer is always right'. However, when considering behaviour, customer care will be more professional and of greater long-term value to all parties if it is provided on the basis that 'the customer always *has* rights'.

For example, if equipment is being misused, then this must be explained, and corrected. If the customer makes a request that is technically unsound, then it is part of the engineer's role to provide a better solution. In neither case is the customer right, and it would be unprofessional to pretend that he is. What does matter is that the customer retains a number of behavioural rights.

He has the right to:

1 Have his views treated with respect.
2 Be listened to.
3 Be treated courteously.
4 Even be wrong.

Earlier, we referred to 'equal rights', and it is important to accept that the engineer also shares these rights, *except for the last one*. As the acknowledged expert, he cannot afford to be wrong.

Consider the examples in 'Behavioural styles' above. Two customers complain, one about the product reliability (or unreliability), the other about prices. In the two recommended responses we can see that the engineers are tactfully implying that the customer is wrong. The engineers have this right to put forward an honest, if conflicting, answer. What is important is that the customers do not appear to be aware of this and are not offended.

From this, we can see that in any situation, both the engineer and the customer have rights. The whole purpose of professional behaviour is that both parties consider their rights have been reasonably satisfied.

Table 10.2 summarizes the situation from the engineer's point of view. The left–hand (vertical) column shows to what extent the engineer's rights have been satisfied with a range from low to high. The same range for the satisfaction of the customer's rights are shown in the top (horizontal) column.

Table 10.2   Behaviour styles

		Satisfaction of customer's rights	
		High	*Low*
Satisfaction of own rights	*High*	Compromising	Determined
	Low	Bountiful	Avoiding

This table shows that *compromising* is the only behaviour style where there is a high level of satisfaction on both sides. That is why it is often referred to as 'win/win'. That does not mean that the other three styles are redundant; occasions when they can be useful are shown earlier in this chapter. Nevertheless, it is important to stress that professional use of avoiding, bountiful or determined behaviour will always contain strong elements of compromise. Extreme use of the 'other three' will almost always be wrong.

Results of questionnaires used on TACK training courses suggest that most experienced service engineers use a mix of all behavioural styles, with a strong bias towards compromising. This is not surprising and it could be claimed that to 'survive' the many, varied situations that occur every day in the service world, engineers have learned to use a mix of styles.

Above all it is necessary to have the confidence and sensitivity to recognize that different approaches are necessary, and that being right or giving in are not the only ways of handling difficult customer situations. Professional behaviour does not just happen; it will certainly require effort from the individual, plus guidance and support from the manager.

Communication

Communication merits a mention here because any person dealing with customers depends upon communication to avoid or solve problems and to establish good customer relationships. More accurately, it should be said that behaviour and communication are inseparable. A good communicator will usually have little difficulty in establishing good customer relationships.

The three golden rules

In the business world emphasis is usually placed on communication as a means of transferring information. When we are considering customer relations, there are three aspects of communication that assume great importance:

1 *Open questions*. These offer the dual advantage of not only obtaining information but also demonstrating an interest in the customer's problems and views.
2 *Listening*. This may be a new experience for many service engineers. Proper listening requires effort and the avoidance of preconceived ideas. One very experienced and highly regarded engineer used to repeat back to the customer everything but the most simple statements. He claimed, 'When I'm wrong they tell me; when I'm right they know I'm listening.'

3 *Thinking*. Think about the customer's point of view. Think about different ways of solving the problem. Think about win/win.

Dealing with difficult customers and situations

The bad-tempered customer

Everyone has a right to lose their temper sometimes, except a service engineer. It costs nothing to apologize if the annoyance is justified. The engineer doesn't have to save face, but he must so act to ensure that the customer doesn't lose face.

The 'knowall'

This might be a situation where 'avoiding behaviour' is required. If the matter is not directly relevant, then it is easy to accept with good grace. If it is relevant, then it is better to listen with some interest before steering the discussion in the correct direction. Open questions asked in a courteous manner could, at worst, reveal flaws in the 'knowall's' opinions. At best, they could elicit additional information.

The watcher or over-anxious customer

Often a manager of foreman insists on watching the engineer's every move. The temptation is to glare, be difficult, or secretive, but this usually makes matters worse and is definitely not good customer relations. The first thing is to accept that he has a right to monitor activities. Perhaps he has had an unfortunate experience with a service engineer in the past, and now refuses to trust anyone of that breed. He might genuinely be curious, or like to know everything that is going on. Whatever the reason, there is unlikely to be a short-term solution.

Accept his presence, treat him as an ally; then when trust has been established, he may well decide that the engineer is now safe to be left alone. If this does not happen, remember the old tag: 'What can't be cured must be endured!'

Untrained operators

There is always the temptation to criticize the standard of employee. A behaviour style verging on the bountiful offers the best approach. Remember, the purpose of service is to fix the machine and try to make sure it does not break down again, irrespective of employee weaknesses.

The sarcastic customer

Because sarcasm can easily be interpreted as humour, it is tempting to use humour in return. If the customer is well known, this might be acceptable. In any other circumstances it is safer to meet sarcasm with a 'straight bat', confident in the knowledge that it becomes increasingly difficult to be 'smart' when the recipient is being sensible and courteous.

Keeping your head at all times

In these paragraphs on behaviour we have attempted to provide a better grasp of a complex problem. We have done this partly by giving understandable labels to some of the various forms of behaviour adopted both by service engineers and their customers. This understanding plus the three golden rules (p. 176) and the determination to avoid reacting to difficult situations will guarantee a much envied reputation for being able to handle customers.

The ideal service manager

A desperate customer who was trying to cope with a major, and potentially expensive, equipment breakdown called the manufacturer to enquire about an engineer whose services he had requested sometime earlier:

Customer: 'You said he would be here any minute, and that was nearly an hour ago.'

Service controller: 'He has a long way to drive, and his name is not Nigel Mansell, you know!'

This story was passed around that particular company as the joke of the month, until it reached the ears of senior management. Not surprisingly, the matter was raised with the service manager, who replied casually, 'You don't understand these customers. Some of them can be downright impossible!'

He was told to change his ways and not to put down a customer – a repetition of such a remark would not be acceptable. As with all business attitudes, good customer relations start at the top. Service managers are too often seen as senior troubleshooters, promoted for their technical expertise. Much of their time is taken up by handling customer complaints that need never have occurred in the first place.

Where should this crisis management end and real management start?

Motivation

Reference to Chapter 3 will demonstrate the importance of motivation in relation to customer care. Service engineers, by choice, are not team players, but the image they enjoy and foster, and the very nature of their work, suggests that their motivational needs are very much in the realms of status and achievement. The astute manager will use this information to promote the challenge of improved customer care.

Direction

All those engaged in the service function should have a clear understanding of their roles, plus the necessary training to carry them out and feed back on their performances. In the preceding paragraphs we have certainly given comprehensive coverage of the ways in which customer service can be improved, together with ideas on training and development. The use of the ASK questionnaire will help to identify areas where improvement is necessary. Performance appraisal and counselling are covered in earlier chapters.

Control

A customer once asked the chairman of a large motor manufacturing company why he never seemed to be in his office. The chairman replied, 'They don't make cars in my office.'

How much time does the average service manager spend out of his office? When he is out in the field, how much time is spent gathering information from a wide range of customers, rather than the favourite few? How much genuine feedback does he receive from customers? In the example of unsafe equipment given on p. 163, the service manager had visited the customer's premises on several occasions without checking the working standards of the engineer. Real control comes from knowing what is going on, measuring results, and identifying problems. Many companies are now recognizing this, and are carrying out scientific surveys of customer attitudes and requirements. What is your company doing?

Correction

If there are problems, then it is the manager's task to solve them. They do not go away, they become crises. Once the information is received, or whenever a problem is identified, any remedial action should be given a high priority. Correction means getting it right next time; it is about results, not about discipline.

Most problems arise from poor selection, poor training, or poor communication. It is no coincidence that these subjects have been given full coverage in this book on customer care.

Customer care and service – footnote

A service engineer arrived in the transport yard of a large company to commission a newly delivered fork-lift truck. He was surprised and annoyed to see a smartly dressed stranger sitting on the truck, attempting to start it. Without a moment's hesitation he told the stranger, 'Don't you know dozens of people are killed every year, fooling around like that? I suggest you get off that truck before you damage it – or yourself!'

Doing as he was told, the culprit climbed down off the truck and went to his office. There he telephoned the purchasing department to congratulate them on their choice of supplier. He then telephoned the fork-lift truck company to tell them how well their engineer had handled a potentially dangerous situation. As managing director of the company, and a knight of the realm, he was certainly entitled to do that. He was reinforcing the view that good service engineers are special people, ideally suited to take a major part in a customer-care policy.

ASK Questionnaire

		Good	Quite good	Poor
Attributes	Confident			
	Helpful			
	Friendly			
	Positive			
	Understanding			
	Diplomatic/tactful			
	Sensitive			
	Sympathetic			
	Enthusiastic			
	Honest			
	Patient			
	Good humoured			
	Objective			
	Courteous			
Skills	Administration			
	Planning			
	Listening			
	Communicating: choice of words			
	speaking clearly			
	Use of time			
	Asking questions			
	Handling objections			
	Gathering information			

(Continued on next page)

ASK Questionnaire *(Continued)*

		Good	Quite good	Poor
Knowledge	Range of products/services			
	Company policy			
	Company systems			
	Applications/limitations			
	Availability (delivery)			
	Pricing structure			
	After-sales service			
	Advertising			
	Geography			
	Competition			
	Financial awareness			
	Your market			
	Client companies			
	Customer needs			
	Buyers/decision-makers			
	Legal requirements			

CRSE/10/1

11 Customer care and the salesman
Alfred Tack

Is the sole objective of a salesman to get an order? Only sometimes, and that sometimes applies to a minority of those who sell direct to householders. Mostly such salesmen are paid by commission only, and the rewards are substantial for sales effected. Their aim is to win an order on the first call, and they don't call back to get repeat orders or to introduce new products, as do salesmen selling consumer goods or industrial products or services.

What salesmen selling to householders rarely realize is that it is just as easy to sell successfully and care for a customer, whether there is repeat business or not, as to use high-pressure methods. Unfortunately too many trainers of such salesmen do not emphasize that the sole objective need not be to get the order. The objective is to fill a need. If the need for additional insurance or financial investment, or an expensive kitchen or bathroom, does not exist, then a sale should not be attempted at that particular time. If the need is there and the householder has finance available, then the salesman can sell with a clear conscience, and still carry out the tenets of customer care by carrying out the principles of professional selling.

None of this applies to the vast majority of salesmen, who call regularly on their customers or prospective customers, or sell through intermediaries – architects, consultants, or doctors. They know that they will ultimately fail if they do not take care of their customers, and if they don't know this, it is not their fault; it is the fault of the trainers. But they can learn the hard way by receiving a poor reception from their customers when they do call back, if they have not shown the care the customers expected.

The objective of salesmen is to satisfy needs and retain customers' goodwill for many years, making sure that they never give an opportunity to a competitor to take business away from them. But in the same way that few people lead unblemished lives, so even the most dedicated companies' customer-caring salesmen can still on occasion forget the basic principles of customer care.

Before we consider how a salesman can give his customers the impression that neither he nor his company really care for them, let us consider another aspect. Not many salesmen will read this book – it is not written for them, it is written for managers and trainers. But it is up to trainers to emphasize *customer losers* to the trainees, and so inculcate these in the minds of the trainees that they will automatically make certain that they do not introduce them when selling.

Only training can implant the right thoughts into the mind of the salesman, and training includes refresher courses and regular bulletins, to ensure that the salesman can remember the basic rules of customer care. Now we can consider some of these customer losers.

Exaggeration

Never persuade a customer to arrive at a decision by making exaggerated claims for a product or service, e.g. that it will fill an exact need when it might only be 70 per cent right for the customers' purpose. This will make certain that at some time in the future there will be a dissatisfied customer.

If a salesman overstates the investment his company is spending on advertising; if a salesman makes a claim that in spite of heavy output from a machine, there will be no breakdowns for years; if he claims, 'You will always get a response from our service department within 24 hours';

and these are exaggerated claims, he will eventually lose out. If he had said, 'It is our objective to give service within 24 hours,' that would have been more reasonable. If he had said, 'It will maintain output so long as it is serviced regularly – I have customers who have operated this machine for years without problems,' he could still get the order without the risk of making any exaggerated claims.

A salesman might claim that his paint, used for the outside of a building, will never discolour. The word *never* is an exaggeration, because all paint discolours after a time.

Customers remember these exaggerated claims, and when the salesman returns for another order he can be told, 'But you said . . .', and that could lose the salesman an order to a competitor. Customer care means keeping to sound selling principles, and never making exaggerated claims.

Promises

Customer care means keeping all promises, large and small, made to those who keep us in business. A survey carried out by Tack Research Ltd, of buyers' likes and dislikes, had *broken promises* high on the list.

There is hardly a buyer who has not heard these claims from salesmen:

- 'I'll call back to see you immediately after delivery, to make sure everything is OK.'
- 'Delivery is normally 8 weeks, but I understand your stock position, and I'll get on to the works director and make sure that you receive delivery in 5 weeks.'
- 'You're so right about advertising; there should be local advertising. I'll take this up with our ad. people, to see that they do get something in your local paper.'
- 'Don't worry, I shall bring the display material myself, to make sure that you get it on time.'

- 'I'll be sure to call to meet your supervisor and foreman, so that they will be quite clear about procedures.'
- 'I'll see you get a demonstration model. It won't cost you a penny, and you can keep it for 14 days. How about that?'

These are some of the promises discovered by our surveys – promises made, but not kept. In some cases the salesmen remember this promise later, and on seeing the buyer will apologize, making some excuse. Typical might be, 'Jones in Despatch let me down; I was so upset when I heard . . .'

This only makes matters worse. At first the buyer has been annoyed with the salesman. Now he has the feeling that the managers at the company's headquarters don't care about him at all. They even let their salesmen down, rather than try hard to supply customers' needs.

Trainers must emphasize that promises must be kept, at whatever cost. If a promise cannot be kept for any reason, then the salesman must immediately return to the buyer and explain what has happened – not by blaming the company manager, but blaming himself for misunderstanding the position regarding delivery, advertising, etc.

Some salesmen continually make promises they are not sure they can keep: changing the nature of a product or delivery would be examples. Ask any works director his opinion, and you will surely be told that too many salesmen are always demanding impossible changes in manufacturing processes, or packaging, which cannot be made.

Another regular request is asking for urgent delivery of a discontinued line.

The salesman always says, 'Oh, I'm sure they can find some if they want to!' But often *they* haven't got any old stock.

Changes in design or packaging cannot be made quickly, to help a salesman keep a promise to a customer –

a promise that good negotiating skills could avoid giving. It is part of a salesman's job to deflect such demands by customers.

On the other hand, head-office managers in all divisions are not necessarily customer-care-minded, and readily blame the salesman for almost everything that goes wrong. They refuse demands that could easily be acceded to, and could satisfy a customer's needs, simply because they are antagonistic to the salesman.

No salesman should make any promises he is not certain that he can keep.

Over- or under-selling

Even a well-trained, experienced salesman sometimes faces a problem that he is not certain how to handle. A novice salesman usually takes the weak way out. A simple example concerns publishers' representatives. No one really knows when a new book by a comparatively unknown author is published whether it will sell or not. It would seem that the publishers' reps should have faith in their company's editors and readers, and therefore try hard to impress on the bookseller that he should take a fairly large number of copies rather than perhaps just half a dozen or less. The bookseller, having so many times landed himself with books that did not sell, would rather take the risk of being out of stock if the book should become a bestseller. His argument is, 'I'll try it out with a few copies, and see what happens.'

What should a representative do?

Try hard, and sell a fair number of copies rather than accept a small order? That is his objective, isn't it? So if he is skilful enough and enthusiastic enough, he may persuade the shopkeeper to place a large order for the new book. But what if the publishers' expectations are not achieved? What if the reviews are few and far between and not all that good? What about word-of-mouth advertising

– the proverbial way, we are told, that bestsellers are created?

The shopkeeper is not amused when daily he looks at large stocks that are not selling, and he is not too happy with the salesman who sold him the copies, nor the publishers that supplied them.

Now let us look at the other side. The salesman takes the easy way out, and accepts a small order. Even good reviews and good publicity may not move many of the books on the shelves. Why? Because good reviews, word-of-mouth advertising, etc., need not send someone rushing to a bookshop to buy. What it does, however, is to motivate those who visit bookshops to remember the reviews, when they see piles of books on display, with perhaps a showcard above indicating a *bestseller*. Two or three books on a shelf josting with dozens of others are sometimes hardly noticed.

Not many people look at every book on a bookshelf. They glance, so that even a well-reviewed book is not noticed if there are only a couple on display. (This of course does not apply to bestselling books by bestselling authors. They create their own demand.)

So the books don't sell well, and when the salesman makes his next routine call, he notices that three out of the six books bought are still on the shelves. The buyer, however, does not consider 50 per cent sales a good investment, so he says, 'They haven't done very well. I won't order any more now. We've only sold a couple of copies.'

That is a dilemma. What should a customer-caring salesman do, when, almost daily, he is faced with this problem? It applies to all areas of selling to retailers or wholesalers.

Should a salesman have faith in his company's product and go all out for a big order? Or should he play safe so that, at least, he won't be criticized when he calls back on that customer?

No retailer is ever going to make a special display when

he has placed a small initial order. When he places a larger order, however, then he nearly always makes a display, and this undoubtedly helps sales.

The answer: on average, a salesman is caring more for his customer when he over-sells rather than under-sells, provided he knows his company will take action to increase the demand for that product. Unfortunately so many companies are very weak on marketing. They believe their products should sell themselves easily – and this so rarely happens.

If a salesman works for a company that pays little heed to personal contact between head office and customer, promotions, incentives, publicity materials, public relations, helping to train staff, or keep staff up to date by means of bulletins, he should never over-sell. But when he receives the right backing, then the general rule is to be enthusiastic, and inspire the buyer to take the maximum quantity that he should be able to sell within a certain time.

Product knowledge

Product knowledge is also high on the list of customer likes and dislikes. Both are closely associated with customer care.

If a salesman lacks complete knowledge of a product, a customer can feel let down if, at some time in the life of that product, acrimonious discussions occur between the supplier's managing director, marketing director, or service manager, because one aspect of the product does not live up to the salesman's claim, or, more to the point, has not been discussed by the salesman at the time of the sale. This need not be due to any sharp practice on the part of the salesman, but to lack of product knowledge. A trainer should tell a trainee to ask himself six questions at regular intervals:

1 Do I know enough about my product (or service) to enable me to talk truthfully, intelligently, helpfully, and factually, to a prospective buyer or prospect?

2 Can I explain the major or minor technical points of my product, so that the buyer will have sufficient knowledge himself to be able to sell it to a third party?

3 As no product is perfect, what factor could a competitor criticize, and, if the buyer passes on that criticism to me, can I prove it to be unfounded?

4 Do I know all the trade terms applicable to my product, so that there can be no misunderstanding at a later date?

5 Do I have such a complete knowledge of the product that I can answer any question the buyer might ask fully and truthfully?

A salesman who believes in the principles of customer care will always strive hard to keep up to date with complete product knowledge. It is up to the trainer to ensure, by verbal or written examination, that the trainee has this knowledge.

Calling back

This subject has been discussed earlier, but it is worth emphasizing, because a call-back can solve problems and misunderstandings, and also create *customer care*. There is an old adage referring to this aspect of salesmanship: 'Never forget a customer – never let a customer forget you.'

The salesman who is so delighted to close a fair-sized order may be sure that at that moment the customer is also reasonably happy at having placed the order. Customers are mostly unhappy before they make a decision, in case they have got it wrong. Once the decision has been made, however, they relax, and are usually pleased that they have shown how decisive they can be. What can upset them later on, however, is the knowledge that before the order was placed, the salesman called almost every week and telephoned regularly, but after the transaction, the salesman is not seen again for months.

The salesman's excuse may be that he is paid to get orders, and if he spends time calling back on all his customers after delivery, he won't have time to open new accounts. Obviously the salesman wouldn't make this excuse if he were selling fast-moving consumer goods, because he knows that the main part of his job is calling back regularly to check stocks and to obtain repeat business. This thinking and application means that eventually his company will make less profit. For various reasons even the best and most competitive of companies will lose customers from time to time. If they are not replaced by new customers, the results will be declining profits. But there will also be declining profits if the salesman doesn't look after his customers.

We all talk nonsense at times, and the salesman who insists that he hasn't the time to call back is certainly one of the nonsense-talkers. Facts show that the average salesman works to only 60 per cent of his capacity (*Tack Survey on Salesmen and Time Management*), but even if a salesman denies this fact so far as he is concerned, good planning by himself and his sales manager will ensure that he has the time for both essentials – calling back and prospecting – but the drive for this 'double' must come from head-office executives. A call-back need not take long; most customers don't want to indulge in lengthy, time-wasting chats. What the customers do want is for the salesman to show an interest in them after a purchase, and to check that all is going well.

Word-of-mouth advertising by customers is far better than any other form of advertising. Customer recommendations will almost certainly lead to more business. Most of all, a salesman must be sure to call back after a customer has let it be known that he feels he has been let down in some way. This is customer care in action.

Many salesmen avoid this duty. It is then up to the sales executive to ensure that they do call back. How? By asking questions and checking reports.

If there is a problem with a customer, then the sales executive must contact the salesman to discover what happened on the call-back, and if there has not been a call-back, then to insist that one must be made. There will be no reason for this if the salesman has been well trained. He will call back automatically, having discovered that caring for the customer means looking after the customer through good times and bad.

The all-round salesman

The all-round salesman is one who is always loyal to his company and strives to do his best for it, and cares for his customers, so that he knows he will always be a welcome caller. Too often a buyer will say to an assistant, 'When Salesman X calls, tell him I'm out! Just get rid of him – he annoys me. He never stops talking, and he wastes my time.'

Remember another selling tag: 'When all things are equal (price, delivery, design, etc.), a buyer usually places his order with the salesman he likes best, and the company he respects most.'

Let us consider the attributes necessary for the all-round customer-caring salesman.

The ambassador

Being a customer-caring salesman does not mean accepting criticism of his company. A salesman sometimes has to act as an ambassador, and an ambassador sometimes has to please the country in which he is

stationed, while, at the same time, explaining diplomatically why his own country is right about some action it
may have taken – but without criticizing the host country
and its leaders.

When a customer insists that he has been promised
longer credit terms, or the guaranteed sole selling rights of
a product, and blames the company's managers, perhaps
as well as the salesman, the latter who knows that he is
right, should not agree with the customer but should
explain, diplomatically, how the misunderstanding has
arisen; he should be determined to leave a satisfied
customer, as well as a satisfied manager. He has shown
customer care through strength. If he gives way all the
time, or blames his company management, he will not be
a caring salesman but a weak salesman, and customers
admire strength rather than weakness. Such strength, used
diplomatically, is a part of customer caring.

The public relations officer

The salesman must be able to keep a customer up to date
with every aspect of his company's activities; this, too,
can give additional confidence to the buyer. Giving a
buyer peace of mind is one aspect of customer care.

Buyers are happy when they learn of a company's
strategy – its worldwide advertising or export business, its
research and development plans, its employment of a
package-designing organization to improve the product's
shelf appeal . . . A company's success in these fields could
help the buyer to arrive at a decision and not to be
concerned that, possibly, he has made a mistake and could
be let down later.

Management consultancy

A management consultant is usually called in to solve
problems. On many occasions a customer will tell a

salesman of a problem he faces – new competition, delayed payments from his customers resulting in a poor cashflow, the problem of training his staff to improve skills, etc. A well-trained salesman acting as a consultant may be able to suggest solutions. A salesman also sometimes has to act as a consultant to prove the real needs of the buyer, for buyers are often not aware of them.

The right mental attitude

Customer care sometimes means more than being punctilious about deliveries or giving rapid service. It can also depend on the relation between salesman and buyer. While it is true that a buyer purchases on value and needs, he is influenced in his decision both before and during a sales presentation by a salesman's actions. When a buyer feels that the salesman is showing him the respect he thinks he deserves, he has the impression that he is dealing with a caring company, caring enough to ensure that its salesman – the vital link between seller and buyer – has been carefully selected and equally carefully trained, resulting in his not wasting the buyer's time.

The impression created by a salesman during a presentation can result in the buyer being confident about dealing with the company, or it can result in a loss of confidence. A trained salesman shows in every move that both he and his company really do care for the customer, because of the quality of their products, their excellent after-sales service, and their willingness to help the customer in every way to be satisfied with his purchase.

So much, then, depends on the salesman's mental attitude, which should be the *right mental attitude*. Because most of the right mental attitudes are well-known to trainers, they are sometimes apt to take them for granted and not to emphasize them. That is wrong!

The right mental attitude must be driven home to every trainee, to ensure customer care.

12 Customer care on the telephone
W. S. Stanley

Managing Director, TACK Training (Overseas) Ltd

When chatting to friends in the living room, talking to neighbours over the garden fence, discussing the latest business drama with colleagues in the conference room, or indeed negotiating a deal with a client, we are communicating not only by the words we use but, almost equally important, by facial expressions and body language. Our neighbour doesn't even need to speak when we tell her how Catherine fell from the ladder in the school gym and lost two front teeth; we can see the concern on her face. We, by our own demeanour, can show concern for a colleague who outlines a stressful situation at a staff meeting; the salesman can show by his sympathetic smile that he appreciates the problem the customer is outlining. We can all show we care in a variety of non-verbal ways.

It is this way of communicating that is denied to us when we use the telephone. It is more difficult then to show our concern, or that we care. It is a great limitation when we use the telephone that neither party can see the other.

You may have experienced an occasion when you have visited your doctor, and while you tell him of your problem, his eyes do not meet yours – he simply carries on signing prescription blanks. You receive the very distinct impression that he has no time for you, that he doesn't care. You may excuse it on the grounds that our doctors are overworked and overstressed. However, we do not make allowances for a stressful situation when we telephone the doctor's surgery and speak to his receptionist. It is not unknown for patients as they hang up the phone to say, 'Why is she always so bloody unhelpful?'

But we mustn't blame the medical profession particularly. A similar scenario is being repeated every day in every industry. When we telephone often, or complain, nobody wants to listen.

Collecting accounts

Sometimes accounts departments show lack of personal awareness, and a great insensitivity when telephoning about an unpaid bill or an overdue account. While accepting that goods and services must be paid for, it is surprising how often those who have to collect accounts criticize the customer before checking that the installation is performing to specification or that goods supplied meet the customers' expectations.

The uncaring caller seems more intent on blaming the customer rather than first asking questions to establish whether there may be something more complex at the heart of the problem. It costs only a moment to say, 'Our invoice was sent out to you 5 weeks ago; perhaps your cheque is in the post to us?' This gives the customer the opportunity of saying either, 'You're quite right, I had forgotten it. It will be in the post this afternoon,' or perhaps 'Yes, we received your invoice some weeks ago, and we have been waiting ever since for your man to return to seal off the end of the ornamental brickwork with silicone.'

Clearly, here is a customer who would quite rightly feel upset if he were subject to a harsh accusation, or, in some way, seemed to be to blame for non-payment of an account. Such phone calls do not help to retain customer goodwill.

Should the customer's response have been, 'Yes, that's right, we haven't paid your account,' it is still wise to adopt a caring, sympathetic approach, such as, 'As you know, our terms are 28 days from date of delivery; am I right in thinking that you have a reason therefore for holding the payment back?' If the response should be, 'Yes indeed! Since the installation we have called you twice to let you know that the V–belt keeps flying off the drive wheel, and twice your service manager has assured us that someone is coming to check it out, but so far no one has come,' at that moment the caller is pleased that his attitude has shown concern for the customer rather than one of conflict. The caller can now say, 'I'm so sorry to hear about that; I knew there must be some good reason why the account hadn't been paid. Leave it with me and I'll chase up the service department. As soon as they have put matters right I'll call you again, just to be sure that everything has been done to your satisfaction.' Later he can call again and say, 'I'm telephoning you this morning as we agreed when last we spoke. I understand from our service department that everything is now running very sweetly. I'm sure you're quite happy, now that the appropriate minor adjustment has been made. You will drop your cheque in the post to us today, won't you?'

It is this more sympathetic type of telephone call that is more likely to result in a customer saying, 'When I finally got hold of the right person, he couldn't do enough for me, to put matters right,' rather than, 'Don't ever deal with XYZ company; they simply leave you in a sort of limbo rather than put things right; but it doesn't stop them howling down the telephone, demanding their money!'

Telephone dislikes

Everyone has his own list of telephone 'dislikes', and many of them are simply an indication that somebody just doesn't care. How many of them, I wonder, have actually happened to *you*?

1 Have you ever been left holding on for what seems ages? A minute of total silence on the telephone can

seem like an age; and when someone eventually does make contact, there is neither an explanation nor an apology for the delay.

2 How many times have you called a number where you know there must be someone at the other end, but the phone remains unanswered?

3 I live about half-way along the Kingston bypass, at either end of which we have excellent DIY shops. This bypass has been described as 'The most dangerous road in England'. I therefore check that an item is in stock at a particular shop before taking my car out on a Saturday morning into quite dangerous traffic. But if no one answers my call, I have to take my chances out on the road. Thinking rationally, of course I know that everybody at the store in question is likely to be very busy, and I don't really expect the young assistant at the top of the ladder taking down a 5-litre can of paint to come running, just because I have telephoned. I do, however, feel that if the management of the establishment cared about its customers, it would have somebody, even if it is only a 15-year-old, still at school, to answer the phone and say, 'May I help you?'

4 A receptionist having a discussion with someone before and while acknowledging the call.

5 A chewing receptionist.

6 When put through to a department, the call is answered with an abrupt 'Sales', 'Accounts', or 'Buying', as if making some kind of challenge. The answer should be 'Good morning – this is Penny Jones Sales Department. How may I help you?'

Always be polite

It is not always possible for callers to know that they may have telephoned at an inconvenient time. Most callers assume therefore that because we have answered the telephone it is all right for them to carry on speaking.

Sometimes it isn't. A caller should always ask, 'Is it convenient to talk to you now about . . .?'

Answering machines

We have to accept that the answering machine is here to stay – and indeed it has proved to be a very useful piece of equipment. The owner of a restaurant who discovers something wrong with his freezer cabinet just as he is closing up at 2 a.m. breathes a sigh of relief when he discovers that he can leave a message on the answering machine of the refrigeration company. He knows, or hopes, that the problem will be put right first thing in the morning. The fact that he has been able to get his message through makes him feel that the suppliers of his refrigerator are concerned to give the best service to their clients.

In contrast, what an irritation it is to call a business number in the middle of the day and *still get an answering machine*! The caller thinks, 'How frustrating! Doesn't anyone care any more?' If the owners' message finishes by saying, '. . . please leave your telephone number and we shall call you back as soon as we return', then that promise must be kept, despite all difficulties.

There is only one annoyance greater than not responding to a message left on an answering machine, and that is not calling back, as promised, after a telephone conversation. That is a sure way of showing lack of customer care!

Concentrate

Do you ever try to do two things at the same time? There are many activities where this is no problem. There is no reason why we should not enjoy a radio programme while we drive along the motorway or weed the flower border. When using the telephone, however, you must concentrate – showing the other party that he or she is the most important person in the world at the moment. If your contact believes that you are only half listening – 'Oh, I'm sorry what did you say?' – the distinct impression created is that of 'don't care'.

When the telephonist connects a call to the wrong department through lack of concentration, or, worse still, accidently disconnects a call wrongly, he/she is not helping the company image. The untrained telephonist who does not appear to know which department would be the most appropriate for your call, or who doesn't seem to know who works where, is surely creating an impression of an uncaring supplier. Rationalizing, companies do sometimes say, 'Give her a chance – it's her first day.' Well, surely she has been provided with an alphabetical list showing the extension numbers of people who are likely to be required on the telephone; and surely she has a list with the names of everybody in each department. If it *really* is her first day, would it not seem sensible to ensure that she has a more established colleague sitting nearby, to help her with her training?

A complaint

Many people on the telephone have a bad habit of saying 'What's your problem?', or, even worse, 'What's *your* problem?' This habit is especially common in people to whom complaints are usually routed. To me this is an indication that they are *expecting* problems and complaints; and they get rather a lot of them! I always feel a compulsion to say – and perhaps I will say it one day – 'I have no problem, but perhaps *you* have!' It is far better for the receiver of the call to say, quite simply, 'How may I help you?'

When you are making a call, some people on the other end preserve their anonymity deliberately by being unwilling to let you know their name. If you do not know whom you are talking to, it is certainly difficult to know what authority they may have or whether they can help you. In addition, if you need to make a further call later on, you cannot ask for that person by name – which means that you have to begin explanations all over again.

The right attitude

If you don't know the answer to a query or problem raised over the telephone, don't bluff or take a chance. If you do bluff, your customer may be satisfied at that moment, but it will prove a very short-term satisfaction indeed. In 3 days, 2 weeks, 4 months, when you are found out, you may lose a customer. Before phoning, check the accuracy of your records and the completeness of your information. Accept that people change, policies change, companies open new departments, ownership changes. When your contacts recognize that you are using accurate, up-to-date information in your telephone conversation, they will know that you care about them.

Take care with words

Be careful of emotive words and phrases. It does not help if you are speaking to an older customer and you say, 'Of course it wasn't so complex in your day, Mr Jones,' 'Times have changed, Mrs Bradley,' or, worst of all, 'In the real world, Mr Jackson . . .'. We *all* live in the real world, and Mr Jackson is more likely to have seen more of it, and to understand it better, than the young caller. So the words you use are not designed to score points off people. Remember the first requirement is to be understood – not misunderstood!

Make notes

Make notes during the conversation, so that nothing is forgotten. If your contact is talking too fast for you to understand clearly what is being said, don't hesitate to say, 'I am writing furiously as you're speaking, Mr Jackson, because what you are saying is too important for me to forget when I write a proposal for you.' The other party will not be upset at the suggestion that what he is saying is so important. The thought may never be put into words, but the impression gained will be that he is in contact with someone who is interested, and cares about what he is saying.

Watch your temper

Earlier I mentioned emotive words and phrases. Be careful not to bring emotion with you to the telephone. If you are angry with one of your children, or irritated by a member of your staff, this emotion can communicate itself to the person at the other end of the line. Stress can cause you to upset a customer. If stress exists, you must control it.

Watch his temper

Of course your contact may be the one who is emotional – angry about something. Because anger is emotional rather than rational, you cannot use logic to deal with it. There is no point in saying, 'Calm down, Mr Jones,' 'I don't have to take this from you, Mrs Bradley,' or 'No need to shout – I can hear you!' It is far better to show a much more caring attitude, to let the other person unburden himself completely – get it 'off his chest'. You can then show your concern – and you *should* be concerned, because you are in danger of losing a customer, or of losing the benefits of a long-standing relationship.

As a young man in the first company I worked for, I remember being impressed at the way a very angry client was handled by a colleague. She said, 'I can understand your being so upset; if that had happened to me I should have been furious!' This immediately placated the customer.

Be courteous at all times

Real courtesy on the telephone is often so unexpected that its mere presence has an immediate and favourable impact, though I don't think anyone will be discourteous intentionally. It is simply a lack of awareness of other peoples' feelings. Courtesy does not mean *icy* politeness; it is not a mechanical function. It is part of an inbuilt, deliberate awareness of the feelings and reactions of other people.

Caring by remembering

Probably one of the easiest ways of all to show our telephone contacts that we care about them is quite simply by *remembering*: remembering what they told us last time – or indeed even a year ago. Remembering the little things that were said in previous conversations, which may not have seemed too important, but our reference back to them in a later conversation shows that we care.

'Oh Miss Page, before you put me through to Mrs Bradley, how was your holiday?' The unspoken assumption is that we *will* be put through to the buying authority, at the same time as we cement the relationship with the all-important secretary. 'Have the builders finished work on the front of your house yet, Mr Jackson?' reminds the customer that we have not forgotten the trauma he told us about in a conversation some 6 weeks earlier.

My advice, almost inevitably, is to make notes, because most of us have fairly poor memories. It isn't that we don't care about what people told us 6 weeks or 6 months ago; it is that we all lead busy lives and it is impossible to remember everything. This philosophy will help your contacts to identify you as a reliable person – you remember your promises and you chase them up on behalf of your client, to ensure that they are kept.

Customer care in action

Remember, your customers may buy from your company, but they talk to your people – they talk to YOU!

Some companies seem to manage quite well without expensively designed literature. Some still sell successfully even though they do not advertise. There are even some companies that manage very well without sales people. However, no company operates without the telephone – and that pre-supposes that there is a friendly, caring person sitting beside it! That is the power of you and your telephone. It is vitally important to your business. Your customers *buy* from your company, but they *talk* to your people.

Here is a summary of the rules by which all of us should be guided when we pick up the telephone:

1 Have your telephone placed within easy reach, and always answer promptly.
2 Let your opening salutation identify you, and offer to help your caller.
3 Try to imagine the caller is in the room with you – and *smile*.
4 Personalize the conversation; use your caller's name.
5 Don't eat, drink, or smoke when telephoning: give each call all your attention.
6 Let the tone of your voice be warm, friendly, interested.
7 If you have to ask your caller to wait, explain why, and when you return, thank him for waiting.
8 Do not contradict; and do not argue.
9 When you promise to call somebody back, *keep your promise*.

10 Always be polite and friendly, and do not interrupt. There is no place in telephone communication for rudeness.
11 Always be prepared to see the other person's point of view. After all, he/she may be right!
12 If you are uncertain of an answer, don't guess; make a proper check.
13 On the telephone, always try to see the object of the call from the other party's point of view.
14 Let your closing phrase be definite, leaving no room for ambiguity.
15 Thank your caller for calling you.
16 Show that you are part of a caring company.

13 Measuring the effectiveness of customer care
Tom Trager MA
Managing Director, TACK Management Consultants

Why measure the impact at all?

Can customer care be measured? Is it worth measuring? Is it really necessary to measure it? Surely if we simply monitor customer complaints, that will provide evidence of our success. Of course this is true, but customers rarely communicate with a company to praise its service or to compare it with its competitors. This information is indispensable if you really want to know how a customer-care programme is perceived by customers. After all, if everyone is making a major effort, they are entitled to know what the impact is. If the impact is positive, they deserve praise and maybe some reward. If there is still some way to go, they should be encouraged to try harder.

Usually when any activity or operation is measured carefully, the results provide information that identifies problems and enables action to be taken rapidly to rectify them. But does this apply to customer care? We were told in an earlier chapter that a customer-care philosophy has to permeate all facets of an organization if it is to be anything but a papering over of the cracks. Surely its impact and results are too intangible to assess. It is not like measuring other aspects of quality, such as the number of faults or defects in a product, when results can easily be correlated with agreed standards and analysed regularly so that improvements or deviations can be monitored.

Successful organizations have to be constantly on the alert to ensure that high standards of customer care are practised at all levels. When standards are high, it is difficult for senior management not engaged in the day-to-day running of the many departments that make up a complex organization to detect any lapses from these standards. They have to employ customer-care audits to gain a thorough understanding of where their company stands in relation to its own standards and those of competitors.

We may think we know all about our business and what customers think of the service we provide, and the manner in which we provide it. Often we are wrong, deluding ourselves into believing that we are operating as customers would wish. Customer-care audits are the means to determine whether our perception of ourselves accords with reality.

What should we measure?

In previous chapters all the components of a successful customer-care programme were identified. This chapter should be regarded as a summary of what has been said before. It contains checklists in the form of questionnaires to assess the impact of customer-care activities on the buyers of a company's products and services, as well as its suppliers.

A customer-care audit has two principal components:

- The first is a continuous review of each individual's customer-care performance against targets that each person sets for him or herself. The quality manager or equivalent carries out this internal audit, and best performances each month or each quarter are awarded small prizes and commendations.
- The second component is an external, objective and independent audit of all the attributes that contribute to customers' satisfaction. Customer satisfaction must be the aim of any customer-care programme, and in this chapter we concentrate on this topic.

A diversity of identifiable attributes contribute to a customer's satisfaction:

1 First and foremost must be the quality of the product or service that has been purchased.
2 Then come all the personal relationship aspects that help to embed a positive image of your company in the customer's mind:
   (a) How effectively is the customer's enquiry dealt with:
      (i) Is the customer put in touch directly with someone who can help?
      (ii) Or does everything need to be explained five times before the right contact is found?
   (b) How responsive/helpful is the contact?
   (c) Do the company's employees appear professional and sharp, or casual and indifferent?
   (d) If there is something wrong with the product or service, how efficiently is the complaint handled?
   (e) Is the product/service delivered on time exactly as promised in the contract?
   (f) Is the invoicing prompt and accurate?
   (g) Are the documentation and administration clear, efficient and supportive?
   (h) If there is an after-sales or maintenance aspect, how well is this organized and carried out?
   (i) If the customer's equipment breaks down, is there a procedure to minimize any inconvenience?
   (j) Does advertising and promotional activity reinforce the buying decision or create dissatisfaction?
3 Whether these tasks are carried out well or indifferently depends on:
   (a) The competence and ability of the staff.
   (b) The quality and frequency of training provided.

No amount of training will convert a group of low calibre, badly managed and indifferent employees into a sharp, customer-oriented organization. Nor will the brightest collection of skilled people be truly effective without relevant, timely and regular training. Companies that have been most successful since the war in the UK, or anywhere else for that matter, always ensure that they employ the best talent available and train them to perfection.

Customers do not buy exclusively from any company, so in order to assess how well your company is performing, you need to know how its competitors deal with their customers or prospects. This constitutes an integral element of the audit.

Suppliers should not be forgotten either, because good supplier relationships are a reflection of a company's concern with caring for its customers. Many organizations seem to take a delight in tormenting suppliers; their techniques are numerous:

1 Keeping suppliers waiting by failing to respond to their telephone calls or written communications.
2 Demanding a quality of product or service that they would never dream of providing themselves, for an impossible price.
3 Never paying on time, or making excuses to delay payment.

The mark of a first-rate customer-care programme is that suppliers receive the same courtesy and professional attention as customers would expect.

Who is responsible for measuring?

All the data needed to measure customers' and suppliers' satisfaction with your company's performance can be collected through surveys. Ideally the person nominated to carry out these surveys should be experienced in consumer research. He or she will have to design the questionnaire, brief the researchers, analyse the results and produce a professional report. If such a person is not available, then a satisfactory alternative is to commission a firm of independent consultants or researchers to carry out the surveys. The benefits of using an independent organization are:

1 Experience.
2 Skills in data input and analysis through computers.
3 A team of expert researchers covering the country.
4 Reliable and valid results.
5 No anxiety about providing unwelcome facts about the company.
6 Ability to explore the real attitudes of your customers, who they may be unwilling to reveal their true feelings to a person with whom they may have been dealing for many years.

Using the results

When the results have been received, the score obtained for each attribute of customer care can form a benchmark against which future scores can be compared. Improvements or backslidings can be highlighted easily, allowing remedial action to be taken if necessary.

When the results are available, they should be communicated to all employees in the organization. Employees should be told how the surveys were carried out, who the respondents were, and the implications of the results on the image, competitiveness and prospects of the company. As all the members of a company are participants in customer care, they must be kept in the picture about everything the company does to apply and measure it, including the cleaning and catering staff. Confining communications to the managers will greatly reduce the value of the exercise, which should be carried out at least once a year.

A point will be reached when the results show a high level of customer satisfaction across all attributes. This is when the customer-care programme has to be redirected to ensure that people do not slip back into former bad habits or sloppy practices. Motivation, morale, training, communication and barrier-free, staff–management relations are the key to sustaining high standards. Other chapters in this book address these subjects in detail.

Having described the audit process in broad outline, let us examine the method.

Appraising competitors

It is always illuminating to assess the quality of competitors' service. Ideally an outside consultant should be asked to contact, say, twenty competitors as a prospective buyer to gain an impression of:

1 The receptionist's knowledge of the organization and his/her ability to identify the person who can respond to a request.
2 Whether that is the right person. If not, how many people does the enquiry have to pass through before being competently dealt with.
3 The interest or enthusiasm of those contacted. Do they seem to care whether you could be a prospective customer?
4 The speed of follow-up if the correct contact is not available.
5 Whether the contact was briefed about the enquiry or not.
6 The quality and relevance of sales literature – it is always worth asking that this be sent.

Customer satisfaction

A typical customer satisfaction survey follows. This questionnaire is not designed for customers who purchase consumer products but rather for the buyers of machinery, equipment, components and professional services.

Customer Survey Questionnaire

Name of respondent _____

Position _____

Name of company _____

1 How long have you been dealing with XYZ Limited?

   No. of years _____

2 What products or services do you buy?

   _____

   _____

3 When did you last buy it/them?

   _____

4 What other products did you consider before buying XYZ's product?

   _____

   _____

   _____

5   What were your reasons for selecting XYZ?

_____

_____

6   Has the product/service met your requirements? In which respects?

_____

_____

_____

_____

7   Are there any aspects with which you are not satisfied?

_____

_____

7.1 What are your reasons for dissatisfaction?

_____

_____

_____

8   What is your opinion of XYZ in
    terms of: *Poor Fair Good Excellent*
    (tick appropriate column)

    8.1   Knowledge and
          professionalism of staff?
    8.2   Receptionist's efficiency in
          handling your enquiry?
    8.3   Responsiveness to requests
          for information or
          assistance?
    8.4   Ability to solve a problem?
    8.5   Quality and frequency of
          after-sales follow-up?
    8.6   Accuracy of invoicing and
          accounting?
    8.7   Delivering on time, as
          promised?
    8.8   Attitudes and
          professionalism of staff:
               Sales?
               Technical specialists?
               Delivery?
               Installation?
               Service?
    8.9   Sales and product literature?
    8.10   Product satisfaction?
    8.11   Willingness and ability to:
               Innovate?
               Upgrade present
               products?
    8.12   Ability to adapt to changing
          circumstances?

9   What major improvements would you like XYZ to make to its products/service?

_____

_____

_____

10   In general how does XYZ compare with its competitors?

_____

_____

11   In terms of the quality of service it provides, how would you rate XYZ out of 10?

1 = low   10 = high   Your rating: _____

12   What is the likelihood of your continuing to buy from XYZ?

1 = low   10 = high   Your rating: _____

Consumer Satisfaction Questionnaire
(Retail)

Name of respondent _____

Address _____

_____

Male/Female

Socio-economic classification (please circle)   AB   C1   C2   DE

1   How long have you been shopping at ABC Ltd?

Number of of years _____

2   How fequently do you shop there? (please circle)

quarterly   monthly   weekly   more often

3   What products or services do you buy?

_____

_____

_____

4   Do you buy these products or services at other stores?

Yes/No

5   Which stores?

_____

_____

6   How frequently do you shop at these other stores

	quarterly	*monthly*	*weekly*	*more often*
Store A				
Store B				
Store C				

7   What are your reasons for shopping at ABC Ltd?

_____

_____

8   Please list these reasons in order of importance

_____

_____

9 What are your reasons for shopping at your other most preferred store (Store A)?

_____

_____

10 What is your opinion of ABC Ltd
    in terms of: *Poor Fair Good Excellent*
    10.1 Location?
    10.2 Car-parking facilities?
    10.3 Opening hours?
    10.4 Range of products and
          services?
    10.5 Quality of products and
          services?
    10.6 Layout and presentation of
          the merchandise?
    10.7 Layout of the store?
    10.8 Prices?
    10.9 Knowledge and
          professionalism of the staff?
    10.10 Staff's understanding of
           the products?
    10.11 Availability of supervisors/
           manager?
    10.12 Helpfulness of the staff?
    10.13 Handling complaints?

11 What aspects of ABC Ltd are you least satisfied with?

_____

_____

12   What major improvements would you like ABC Ltd to make?

_____

_____

_____

_____

13   In terms of the quality of service it provides, how would you
     rank ABC Ltd out of 10?

1 = low   10 = high   Your rating: _____

14   What is the likelihood of your continuing to shop at ABC?

1 = low   10 = high   Your rating: _____

For buyers of consumer products in retail outlets the
emphasis has to be on the quality of service provided by
such outlets. An outline consumer satisfaction survey
follows:

Sample size and composition

A sample of buyers that accurately reflects a cross-section
of products and services sold in the last 12 months should
be selected. If you have a large customer base, a sample
size of between 10 per cent and 20 per cent should be

sufficient to enable the results to be sub-divided by, for example:

(a) Location.
(b) Value of purchase.
(c) Type and size of enterprise.
(d) Type of product or service bought.

For companies operating in specialized niche markets, the sample size may have to be proportionately larger, but may not be sufficient to produce a meaningful break-down of results into sub-groupings.

Sooner or later, when carrying out such a survey, the researcher will encounter a customer who, though still loyal, has had one particularly unfortunate experience in dealing with your company. The researcher should ensure that the full reasons for dissatisfaction are explored, identifying who was responsible and why inadequate follow-up action was taken to remedy the problem. Careful note should be taken of such cases, and a separate, confidential report issued to the directors.

Lapsed customers

Lapsed customers should be included in any survey. It is important to find out why these customers ceased buying from your company. Lapsed customers constitute a pool of potential customers if their confidence can be regained. The mere act of carrying out a survey of their reasons for ceasing to buy from you often indicates that your company is serious and is taking positive action. After the survey, the sales department should take the opportunity to follow up and re-establish contacts.

It is surprising how often insufficient effort is made to find out why a customer has lapsed; sometimes a sales person may believe the customer is so dissatisfied that it would be embarrassing to call on him or her again. Yet when an outsider contacts the customer, he/she is relieved to have the opportunity to put his/her side of the case. Sometimes there is a profound wish to mend fences and renew contact. This applies particularly if dissatisfaction arises from a clash of personalities, and one of the parties has since left.

Follow-up surveys

At least once a year, follow-up surveys should be conducted. These should be based on interviews with about 85 per cent of the original sample, supplemented by customers who had not been interviewed previously, resulting in a total sample of the same size and composition as the original survey sample. Tracking performance over time encourages the process of continuous improvement, raising the standard a little each time to attain that perfect score – 100 per cent customer satisfaction.

14 Time management
Eric Pillinger BA, DMS, FCCA

*Managing Director, TACK Training International Ltd
and Director, TACK Industries Ltd*

Too much to do – too little time!

That's the viewpoint of the vast majority of managers I meet. Typical comments are:

- 'How can I ever catch up?'
- 'I'm up to here with work' (with a karate-type blow to the forehead indicating that they are not far short of bursting point!)
- 'I always have to come in at weekends.'
- 'I feel like I'm on a treadmill.'
- 'The phone never stops ringing.'
- 'I'm at breaking point, what can I do?'

We all identify with some of these feelings some of the time. Yet here we are reading a book that suggests more activities, more responsibilities and apparently more effort. Is it all possible? A good manager has never done everything he or she would like to do. Yet with professional time-management methods we can all keep control of our workload and ensure that we achieve good results without working 7 days a week. Good time management can help 95 per cent of all those managers who feel they cannot cope effectively. But of course we have to apply self-discipline. Nothing in this chapter, on any course, or in any time-management book, will ever work for somebody who does not have the discipline to apply the principles that they know they ought to be applying! So be of good cheer! If you will put into practice all the methods outlined in this chapter, you will most surely find the hours needed for a successful customer-care policy.

Keep it simple

You will remember that in Chapter 7, Quality, Brian Moss insisted that quality means 'satisfying needs' and not going overboard and giving the customer more than is actually required. The same applies in self-organization, namely, to those very elaborate 'filing systems-cum-diaries'. Naturally a diary is essential, and it should always be allied to a task list and sometimes to a daily action plan (Figures 14.1 and 14.2). A diary, a task list and a pocket notebook will meet most people's needs, when combined with a precise daily action plan for particularly high pressure days, or days when there are a lot of appointments. If you do want a 'personal organizer', then do get one of the simple ones that does not require a degree in mathematics or logic to understand and use it! Certain people can get tremendous value out of a slightly more sophisticated personal organization system, but many people who spend a lot of money on them simply find they are owners of the world's most expensive pocket diary (which won't even fit in a pocket!).

Work to priorities

Unless you work to priorities you will, undoubtedly, use your time less effectively than you could. But you may well say, 'How can I work to priorities? Surely it is essential to get all the urgent jobs done first?' Not so! If you try to do all the urgent jobs first, you will find that you have got so many urgent jobs that you need to have a system working out degrees of urgency to decide which are more urgent than the other urgent jobs! To achieve objectives in the best interests of your company, you must tackle the *important* jobs first, i.e. those that have high *value*.

All managers are paid to deal with matters of importance that relate to the profitability, growth and security of the company. Important tasks may relate to

DATE _____

No.	Outstanding task	Priority	Delegate?	When?
1				
2				
3				
4				
5				
6				
7				
8				
9				
10				
11				
12				
13				
14				
15				
16				
17				
18				
19				
20				
21				
22				
23				
24				
25				
26				
27				
28				
29				
30				

Figure 14.1 Task list

DAY _____

DATE _____

Floating tasks, which must be done today	Notes, ideas, reminders, messages, etc., which arise during the day
1	
2	
3	
4	
5	
Fixed tasks or appointments (or tasks that you want to make fixed)	
8.00	
8.30	
9.00	
9.30	
10.00	
10.30	
11.00	Floating tasks or time fillers which could (or should!) be done today
11.30	
12.00	People: _____
12.30	
1.00	
1.30	
2.00	
2.30	
3.00	Phone: _____
3.30	
4.00	
4.30	
5.00	
5.30	
6.00	Paperwork: _____
6.30	

Figure 14.2 Daily action plan

training, new product development, meeting customers, cost control, or cashflow. These are all matters that have high value or high cost (if not done satisfactorily). Such tasks need concentrated thinking and planning, and they must have sufficient time allotted to them so that they can be done properly. So many apparently urgent tasks are not really that urgent, and maybe not at all important or valuable.

Even a request made by a senior manager may not be truly important; if there are more valuable priorities to be done, you may even discuss his request and jointly agree that it can wait for a while. But never forget that the boss is the boss and that, at the end of the day, if you want to succeed in business, you have to do what he asks you to do!

When planning your day, you must find time to carry out both important and urgent tasks, but your priority must always be to complete the important (i.e. high value or high cost) tasks first at the expense of all else. If you keep putting off high value tasks until all the apparently urgent ones are done, then you will probably fall into the trap of leaving them all to the last moment and then doing them inadequately, having spent all your time doing urgent trivia brilliantly!

The criterion to determine priority is the ultimate value of the task. It doesn't really matter if you short cut on low-value tasks: you can do them in a hurry, you can do them unsatisfactorily, or you can delegate them.

So apart from giving too high a priority to apparently urgent tasks that are 'making a lot of noise', how else do we distort our priorities? Apart from the 'boss distortion', which is mentioned above, another very common source of problem is 'fun distortion'. That means doing the things that you enjoy because you enjoy doing them rather than because they have a high pay-off. Very often the things we enjoy doing do not have a great value, even if they are easier than the tasks that actually yield high returns.

It's amazing how often managers who claim to be impossibly busy can find time to go out to a business lunch, to visit an interesting exhibition, or to go and see one of their colleagues for a chat about something that isn't very important. This all comes back to my original point about self-discipline. To work to priorities does require self-discipline, as well as rational analysis of what needs to be done and how important each of those tasks is.

Delegate whenever possible

Always delegate to others what others can do as effectively as you, and, presumably, at lower cost, because they earn less than you. You can delegate simple tasks that are not particularly challenging, and save yourself a lot of time; you can delegate major projects that provide people with challenges, provide them with development opportunities, and still save yourself a lot of time; or you can delegate routines – those tasks that come up once a week, or once a month or once a quarter and take up a certain amount of time whenever they crop up. If you can delegate these last to other people, then you save the time each time that routine occurs.

When you delegate tasks to other people, it is often very tempting to check what they are doing very, very carefully, just in case something is going wrong. While it is sometimes necessary to check closely the results of delegated work, e.g. if the cost of an error is very high, if you insist on checking everything, it negates all the benefits of delegation. Firstly, it negates all the time-saving benefits to you, because if you are checking everything, you might as well do the job yourself. Secondly, and maybe more importantly, it negates the motivational and development benefits to your subordinates – if you are all the time hovering over them, watching what they are doing and checking their results, they feel neither motivated nor flattered.

Rules for delegating

1 Make sure that your subordinate has the capability to do the job effectively and has sufficient time to achieve it without excessive stress. This may obviously call for training, without which delegation cannot be effective.
2 Always explain fully the purpose of the assignment, and spell out exactly the benefits to the company, so that the subordinate will feel proud to take on the task and will feel motivated to do it well.
3 Communicate very clearly what it is that you actually require. Delegate the 'end result' rather than the process.
4 Clarify the time and resources you are allowing the person. You should always set a time deadline; you should always make it clear whether the person has to do everything himself or herself; and you should always make it clear whether or not they can spend money getting the job done. If there is any doubt about this at all, it's never a bad idea to confirm it in writing.
5 Monitor the assignment as unobtrusively as possible. It is still your responsibility to see that the task is satisfactorily completed, and although you delegate, you cannot abrogate the duty of making sure that the work is done well and on time. Always try to show regular interest in the task. Nobody feels fully motivated if given a delegated task they think their boss has forgotten about – the suggestion is that it was not sufficiently important for him to follow up.
6 Make it clear whether or not you wish the subordinate to come back to you or somebody else if he has problems. Explain it is not a sign of weakness if a problem cannot be resolved without help. Equally, if your philosophy is that people have to 'sink or swim' on a delegated task, then make it very clear that that is your philosophy. But you must accept that if you adopt this strategy and the person makes an error, you still have to support them.

7 If everything goes right, then give the person the credit. Probably publicly. This recognition and thanks is in itself a form of reward. If the person has undertaken a major challenge and completed it satisfactorily, you may wish also to give him some sort of tangible reward for his achievement. But the most important thing is that subordinates know that to take delegated work and do it well is recognized and rewarded in some way.

8 If things go wrong, avoid heavy criticism. Mistakes will happen. Remember that it's part of your responsibility, and so if you are blaming the subordinate for things going wrong, you are also blaming yourself. If there are errors on delegated tasks, then try to turn them into learning opportunities. Ask 'What have we learned?' Ask 'How shall we ensure that this does not happen next time?' Turn it into something positive rather than something negative. There is a managerial bird known as the 'yellow-bellied credit snatcher', whose strategy is to steal the credit if something goes right and allocate the blame totally to the subordinate if things go wrong. If you want to motivate your people to take delegated work, avoid this sort of behaviour!

Control your paperwork – don't let it control you

Many of us waste too much time on paperwork – reading it, re-reading it, filing it, shuffling it, losing it, rewriting it, etc.! Even with the growth of electronic mail systems, paperwork does not disappear completely; you simply have a mixture of electronic paper and ordinary paper!

So do keep your paperwork physically under control – nothing is more depressing than having pieces of paper and piles of junk lying all over your office, your desk and your window sill. Try to handle each bit of paper once; try to resolve it or action it the first time you touch it. This isn't always possible, but it's an excellent objective to have. Don't file too many things – use the wastepaper bin as much as possible. Use the technique of writing on paper by hand if a comment is needed, and passing on the original memo with the handwritten additions – these days there is no need at all to have lengthy memos typed out. Some things you do handle formally, e.g. a circular to a lot of people in the company, or a report to senior management, but very often the 'scrawl and send' technique is more efficient and more personal, and these days it is quite acceptable.

Identify your 'time fillers' and use them skilfully and selectively

There are many tasks that you have to do which can be efficiently completed in small time gaps of 5, 10 or 15 minutes. These we call 'time fillers'.

You use time fillers to make those small time gaps productive. Most people tend to waste the 5 minutes between meetings or the 10 minutes before lunch, because they always say to themselves that it is not worth starting anything within such a short space of time.

Try to change you attitude towards these time gaps. View them positively as opportunities to make that quick phone call, to write that short memo, or to do that bit of reading. These small tasks have to be done some time, and it's much better to do them in small time gaps than to use large chunks of time to do lots of different time fillers.

Always carry time fillers with you when you travel. It doesn't matter how you travel – by train, by plane, by car, by underground, by taxi – there will always be opportunities to do work while you are travelling. For instance, if you drive somewhere for an appointment, you always have to aim to arrive at least 15 minutes early because of unpredictable delays. As you sit in the reception area of that large office block waiting for your appointment, if you've got some trade journals with you, then you can read them instead of reading the magazines that happen to be positioned in the reception area. When you travel by train, you can do creative work because you know you are not going to be interrupted by the telephone. When you travel by plane, it is fairly predictable that you will be delayed either in an airport or in the plane, and although having work with you does not make the waiting any more acceptable, at least it makes it more productive.

Just think of it, if you could use three 5-minute time gaps a day that you presently waste then over the period of a year, that would add up to something like 1½ weeks of extra productive work.

Making appointments

It is obviously far better for your time management if visitors come to you rather than you going to them – you do not have to worry about the travelling time and you can work effectively right up to the moment they arrive. The only drawback to having the meeting in your office is that it is slightly more difficult to terminate it when you've had enough. If you go to the other person's office, then it's easier to leave.

If people are coming to you and you wish to make them very prompt, you can always try the unusual technique of making an appointment at one of the non-traditional times, e.g. 4.10, 4.50 as opposed to 4.30 or 5.00. The fact that you suggest a very precise time suggests to them that you are a very precise person, and this motivates people to be precise themselves.

When you are the one doing the travelling to the other person's office, it is a very good idea to try and arrange a 'floating' start time for the meeting. Rather than saying you will arrive at 2.00 or at 2.30, you say you will arrive some time between 2.00 and 2.45, and you ask whether this is acceptable. The worst the other person can say is 'No, you have to tell me exactly when you're coming.'

But surprisingly often they will say that they will be in the office anyway over that period and any time between 2.00 and 2.45 is acceptable.

The big advantage of this to you is that you do not have to leave a safety margin for your travelling time. If you have to get somewhere at a precise time, then you have to allow a safety margin. If you already have the safety margin built into the start time of the appointment, then you do not need to worry.

I know that many sales people will say that if they don't make a very precise time, their customer will keep them waiting. But my experience is that customers usually feel they have the right to keep you waiting anyway if you are visiting their premises, so you might as well be kept waiting with a floating start time as with a fixed start time. And if you take time fillers with you, so that your waiting time is not wasted time, then you don't have so much of a problem. For sales people who are trying to fit as many appointments as possible into a fixed period of time, if you agree floating start times with your customers, you will generally find you can squeeze in, with safety, one extra meeting per day without running the risk of being unacceptably late for any of them.

The ever-open door

Often managers are proud of the fact that they have an open door, and anyone can walk in. But an open door can mean more time wasted.

The manager will continually have to deal with matters of little importance, because Lucy wants to complain about John, Bill wants to talk about a memo he has received with which he doesn't agree, or Arthur wants to ask for time off, etc. Remember, 'Anyone can see me at any time' is not something to boast about. It is inefficient. Important meetings should always be by appointment, so that you can devote enough time to them. The rest of the time there is nothing wrong with having a 'closed door policy' sometimes and an 'open door policy' when you wish.

Letters, memos, reports

Many executives are now doing most of their own typing. Portable computers are available at an acceptable price and word processing software is now sufficiently sophisticated that an unskilled typist can produce good quality work in a reasonably short time. So if you are at all that way inclined, the most cost-effective approach to letters and memos may be to do them yourself.

If you are not prepared to turn yourself into an amateur typist or if you have not got the budget for a portable computer and printer, then you are left with two other alternatives – either to dictate to a secretary or into a recording machine or to draft the memos out longhand and pass them on to a secretary. If you are one of those people to whom words come very easily and whose spoken communication can easily be converted to written communication, then by far the most cost-effective thing to do is to dictate on to tape and then pass the tape to a secretary who can process the work at the most convenient time. If, after practice, you find you cannot make tape-dictating work, then it may still be possible to be effective at personal dictation. But if you do not have the luxury of a secretary who can take dictation, then you have to revert to the traditional longhand 'draft', which is then passed on to somebody else to type. Even though it obviously takes longer to write things down than to speak them, for many people longhand still is, in the end, the most effective way of getting things down on paper.

Some people can write quickly, some not so quickly, but it is important to ask yourself how vital the communication is. If it is a letter or a proposal to a customer, then it is worth agonizing over the detail and drafting out the letter or report to be 99.9 per cent accurate and correct. If it is only for internal consumption, then resist the temptation to make it too word perfect, because in the end, all that memo is trying to do is to communicate information.

However, it is very important to consider who the recipients are. If, for example, you have a managing director who puts great store by very neat, clear communications and judges somebody's competence on the neatness of his or her memos, then it is pretty important to allow for the boss's preferences! If, on the other hand, your company's culture is that the message is more important than the appearance, then for many internal communications you do not need to type or word process them at all. Simply write out a message longhand (if possible in legible hand!) and simply photocopy your handwritten note and send it around to everybody.

In my experience there is no completely right answer when it comes to deciding how much paperwork you should send out to people – if you communicate everything to everybody then you will get complaints that there is too much paperwork going around the organization. If you cut back on this paperwork and don't always tell everybody everything they need or want to know, then they will complain of poor communication!

Mail your voice

These days one way of cutting back on letters and memos is to use the various technological aids that are available – particularly voice mail. Many people now have answering systems connected to their telephones, or they have a recorded message bank somewhere. It is so much quicker just to pick up a telephone and talk to a recording device for a minute or so than it is to write out even a short memo. The more communication you can do by voice mail rather than by paper (or even by electronic mail), the better.

Meetings

Are meetings a waste of time or are they an essential part of the management process? There is no complete answer, because there is no typical meeting.

Some people call too many meetings; some people call too few. Some people let them go on too long; other people bulldoze meetings through so quickly that there is no time for discussion of even important matters. Some people call far too many people to their meetings; other people leave out important people, so they don't get consulted. Some people have a very structured meeting, where the agenda is so rigid that people's creativity is stifled; other people run meetings with no agenda at all, so that everybody goes around in circles and achieves nothing.

The only correct strategy on meetings is to have the minimum number of meetings with which the business can satisfactorily be run, but to make sure that each one of them is well planned, well structured and well run, so that good effective decisions, which can contribute to the business, are made.

There are only two valid reasons for having meetings. One of them is to communicate information and the other one is to make decisions. In my experience it is better not to mix the two types of meetings. If you have an information meeting, then simply call together everybody who is needed, present the relevant information as quickly as possible and then allow adequate time for questions. Do not get into making decisions at meetings like this.

If the objective of the meeting is to make one or more decisions, then here are some suggestions on planning and running 'decision–centred' meetings:

1 All the items on the agenda should be phrased as questions requiring a clear decision to be made on how to achieve a particular objective. If you can't phrase the

agenda in terms of questions, then you haven't thought it through fully. Try this discipline next time you are planning a meeting, and you will find that it takes you longer to draw up the agenda but it saves an enormous amount of time during the meeting.

2 The agenda items, i.e. the questions, must be arranged in the order of the importance of the decisions to be made. Always consider the important decisions early on in the meeting and leave the trivial decisions to the end of the meeting. This way, if you don't finish the agenda, all the things that you leave unfinished are fairly unimportant. Alternatively, if you decide to bulldoze your way through the agenda to get the meeting finished on time, then you are only bulldozing the small decisions and not the important ones! Equally, it means that everybody's brainpower is at its best when you are tackling the toughest decisions.

3 Keep people on track as much as is reasonable. You will never stop people from straying off the point a little bit, and it would probably stifle creativity to do so. So while you should not be too rigid in controlling discussions, you should always keep people on track by asking regularly 'What is the relevance of this to the question we are addressing?'

4 At nearly every meeting there is at least one compulsive talker and at least one silent listener. The meeting leader's job is to encourage the silent listener to express his opinions and to stop the compulsive talker from monopolizing too much of the time. This is not easy, as very often the compulsive talkers have a lot of worthwhile points tucked away in their torrent of words! Equally the silent listener may have a lot of worthwhile information to say, so everybody must be given equal opportunity to express their opinions, even if they don't actually use that opportunity. But don't forget that very often it is the chairman himself who is the compulsive talker and who is the worst offender of all in helping meetings to overrun!

5 At the start of a meeting try to lay down a definite finishing time. The meeting does not have to be short (although it is probably better if it is), but it must have a definite time at which it will finish. This focuses people's minds marvellously as the finishing time approaches.

6 Keep minute-taking to an absolute minimum. In fact I don't even recommend the use of the word 'minutes', because this in itself suggests lengthy, verbatim reports of everything that has gone on. Very much better only to record the decisions that were made at the meeting, the name of the person who is responsible for implementing each decision, and the target date. There is no reason at all why you cannot write these decisions down during the meeting itself, photocopy them at the end of the meeting and hand out the meeting summary straight away. Then all anyone has to do is to look for their name on the minutes and focus on their particular responsibilities.

7 Restrict attendance to those whose presence is essential. Do not waste the time of other people, who may ask to 'sit in' or who may feel affronted because they have not been invited to attend. Unless people are actually concerned with the decisions to be taken, do not bother to invite them, although it is always politic to explain why not. If people are concerned with only part of the agenda, then they do not need to come to the whole meeting. Invite them just for that period of time which relates to their subject, and then they can go.

8 Try to avoid deferring a decision by passing it on to a sub-committee or sub-group to make that decision – this is usually just an excuse for procrastination. But it is perfectly all right to make a decision in principle and refer to a sub-group for implementation – that is very efficient.

9 The best way to follow up the summary of the previous meeting is for the chairman to do it before the next meeting begins. The traditional 'going through the

minutes of the last meeting at the beginning of the next meeting' is a recipe for disaster. All that happens is that you relive the last meeting. The chairman should check with each person whether or not they have implemented the decisions allocated to them previously; then all he needs to say at the beginning of the next meeting is 'I have checked through the minutes of the last meeting and everything has been completed except for . . .'. This takes a couple of minutes, and then everybody can get on with the new decisions.

If these rules are adhered to, hours, even days, may be saved each year. But the best time-saver of all is to keep meetings to a minimum. Ask yourself these questions when deciding to hold a meeting:

(a) What may we get out of the meeting that could not be achieved in other less time-consuming ways?
(b) Am I quite sure this meeting is necessary and has not been called simply to air my own views or to boost my own ego?

A very good test of executive efficiency is how few meetings you hold rather than how many.

Reading

Every week managers receive reading matter of all kinds – direct mail shots, brochures, books, magazines, trade papers, government forms, government reports – which they cannot find the time to read. Is the answer to this time-consuming problem to learn speed reading? Well, anything that helps you to read articles more quickly is obviously worth doing, and some people do find formal speed-reading techniques to be useful. But for the majority of managers I believe they are quite unnecessary, as there are two alternatives.

The first is to pass on to others the task of reading through the magazines you receive, asking them to mark up those sections that will be of interest to you. This of course is a form of delegation, and so you have to give some training, as you do with all delegation. But if you tell people what topics to look out for and you tell them to use their initiative in highlighting the things that will be of interest to you, then this is a very good time-saving form of delegation, which will very rarely cause you to miss out on anything important.

The second alternative is to teach yourself to 'scan'. You do not have to have a photographic mind to scan through a page and remember the main facts. You may miss an item now and again, but don't worry. Most things are repeated over and over again in different articles and in different media, and what you miss one day in a newspaper or report will surely come up again shortly in another trade journal.

Naturally this concept of scanning does not apply to those in the legal profession or to accountants, who may have to read line by line, dot by dot, comma by comma. But it does apply to most managers in business. If you develop the scanning habit by practice, you will find that, although it is not perfect, it is a very effective way to save time when faced with a weekly mass of documents that have to be read.

For example, I have in front of me a business magazine, and I am looking at an article headed: 'Can you afford to pay your workers in cash?' The first line reads: 'We are gradually moving towards a cashless society.' Obviously the copy is going on to refer to the fact that most companies should pay employees by cheque instead of cash. Most managers know the arguments for and against this procedure, but for all that, in case anything new has come up, the article should be scanned. The first fifty lines or so need not be read, since they only provide statistics of various companies who do, or do not, pay by cash. I therefore begin reading half-way down the first column: 'Why are we behind other countries in what is obviously a safer, more modern way of paying people?' The next line which attracts my attention begins: 'The principle of the employee's right to choose was restated in the Payment of Wages Act 1960.' That's enough information for me!

My eyes stop at the next headline: 'Bank Giro'. I read some twenty lines, giving the viewpoint of bankers relating to payment through giro. Then I skip, until, finally, I read the summing up – the last twenty lines. The total article contains several thousand words, but by scanning it I have been able to take the meat out of it, reading possibly only 500 or 600 words.

If I had discovered, on scanning through, that the subject matter was such that I could learn more by studying it carefully, I should of course have read it line by line. But in most articles this is quite unnecessary. Scanning will tell you all you need to know.

Why not test your scanning abilities? Scan through an article or a report, then ask an associate to question you on it. Carry out this exercise regularly, and you will find scanning easy and rewarding. There are those with pedantic minds who read every word on every page of every sheet of paper placed before them. There are others, such as judges, professors, scientists, who obviously have to ponder over every word. Business managers need only scan.

Talk, don't write

Like the compulsive talker, there are some compulsive letter- and memo-writers. All too often memos are written for the wrong reasons: for example, when Manager A wants to criticize Manager B or his department for something; or when Manager X wants to correct some aspect of Subordinate Y's behaviour; or when Manager Z wants to play politics and send copies of complaints or requests to a large number of people at different levels.

Whenever you feel tempted to write to someone on a sensitive matter, think twice before doing it. It will probably be both quicker and more effective to telephone them or go and see them. You can always back it up in writing if necessary.

It is usually more cost-effective to speak to people, because it gets the whole discussion over and done with at one time – if you write a memo, then they have to reply, you have to reply to their reply, and the whole thing drags on. Also it is much easier to annoy people on paper than it is to annoy them face to face. So, especially on sensitive matters, remember the good old rule 'talk, don't write'.

'But I work best like this'

Many managers waste time and effort because they are personally disorganized and have a cluttered desk, cluttered briefcase, cluttered drawers and a cluttered personal computer disk. When tackled, every such manager always claims to know exactly where everything is, and to keep his task list in his memory, where he finds it 'easier to focus on priorities'.

If you are one such, then by all means kid other people, but please don't kid yourself! No one works effectively when surrounded by chaos; or in the unlikely event that they do, they would work even more effectively if they got everything together. Try to keep an orderly office if you want to keep an orderly mind. Many of us waste too much time looking for things, forgetting things, or working on the wrong things.

When you are away . . .

Every manager has experienced the stress of returning from a business trip abroad or a holiday to find work has piled up. Most managers have an assistant or secretary who can do much to clear up that backlog if only they are allowed to do so.

Many managers say 'Don't touch anything until I return'; other managers give no encouragement to their team to do anything or make any decisions in their absence. This is absurd. If a manager doesn't have a good assistant or secretary, then his training scheme has broken down, in which case there is no alternative to having a stressful situation on his return.

At least one of your subordinates should be able to do his or her best to carry out routine tasks, even making decisions in your absence within certain budgetary limits. Your objective is to have as little as possible left over for your return when you do get back from a trip or a holiday.

If you develop your subordinates and encourage them to use their initiative, then, although they will sometimes make mistakes, they will save you a lot of time and also a lot of stress. The most important thing for you when you get back from 2 or 3 weeks away is to be able to spend the first 1 or 2 days back going around speaking to people and listening to them. You should not be panicking over all the small jobs that were not done in your absence!

How about the 'may be important' jobs?

Every manager has the responsibility to invest a certain amount of his or her time working on the 'three I's' of management – ideas, innovations, improvements. A certain percentage of your time has got to be devoted to thinking creatively, looking for new ideas and planning improvements in the way that you and your department work.

Nobody knows what percentage of your time should be allocated to these activities, because nobody knows how successful they will be. But, for example, going to exhibitions, going to conferences, reading journals,

244 Profitable Customer Care

meeting people for an informal chat, seeing sales people –
all of these come under the category of activities that 'may
be important'.

If you are under pressure, it's tempting not to spend
time in these areas unless they cover things you enjoy
doing, e.g. most managers will find time to go away for a
2- or 3-day conference in a comforable hotel at an exotic
venue, but those same managers, if phoned for an
appointment by a sales person, are very likely to say they
did not have the time to spare half an hour to listen to his
ideas!

So although you must speculate some of your time on
the 'three I's' part of your job, be sure to do so
consistently and objectively. Spend your time where you
are most likely to get a good return on your investment,
and not just on the things that you enjoy doing.

Planning your day

Every working day you have to decide which tasks you
are going to give priority to. Note, I say you must *decide*
which tasks you will give priority to, rather than have
priorities thrust upon you.

During most days certain tasks *must* be carried out. It is
important to focus on these 'musts', because they will
undoubtedly have a high value or a high cost attached to
them. You must do them by the end of the day,
regardless.

After that, consider which tasks *should* be completed
during the day. They may be of some importance or some
urgency, and should be done if at all possible; but it is not
disastrous if they are rolled forward. Identify these – it is
desirable to get them done, but if you go home without
having done them, then you need not have a sleepless
night.

Finally, consider those tasks that could be completed
during the day. They may be neither of great importance

nor of great urgency, but, if convenient, they should be carried out because they are of some value. Unlike some people I do not believe in dismissing these 'coulds' totally. The cumulative effect of a lot of small jobs done well can be very great – sometimes it is only to foster goodwill in someone else, or sometimes it is only to glean a little bit of information. While it is not important necessarily to do all these tasks or to do them 100 per cent perfectly, each one has a small value that can help to improve your effectiveness.

So every morning (or the evening before if you prefer) review your 'musts', your 'shoulds' and your 'coulds', along with your fixed appointments for the day. You can then produce a reasonably flexible plan that gives you the best opportunity to meet all your objectives during the day with the minimum stress. So if you have a tough day ahead of you, try drawing up a daily action plan the night before (see page 226).

Conclusion

When you put these time-management procedures into practice, you will not only find the time to do the administrative part of your job properly, you will also find more time to carry out your leadership responsibilities.

Being conscious of other people's feelings and concerns is part of a company's culture. It is just as important to care for your staff as it is to care for your customers. Make sure you have the time to advise and counsel them when they are facing difficulties or have personal problems. You will need time to counsel, direct, and develop the members of your team for their future responsibilities as well as their present roles. When you care for your own staff, you can expect them to care for your customers and to respect you. Like everything else in business, leadership takes time. But good leadership is the basis of good customer care.

The aim of this book has been to give you some ideas about caring more for your customers, so that your customers will care more for you and your company – whatever the economic conditions and whatever the competition. You have to succeed through your people, but before you can manage your people, you have to learn to manage yourself. Good time management solves many problems.

Index